Light Up Your Life

Light Up Your Life

And Keep It Lit!

ROBERT T. GARDNER JR., MSW

Copyright © 2017 by Robert T. Gardner Jr., MSW.

Library of Congress Control Number:		2017906242
ISBN:	Hardcover	978-1-5434-1820-0
	Softcover	978-1-5434-1819-4
	eBook	978-1-5434-1818-7

All rights reserved. No part of this book may be reproduced or transmitted in any form or by any means, electronic or mechanical, including photocopying, recording, or by any information storage and retrieval system, without permission in writing from the copyright owner.

Any people depicted in stock imagery provided by Thinkstock are models, and such images are being used for illustrative purposes only. Certain stock imagery © Thinkstock.

Print information available on the last page.

Rev. date: 08/30/2017

To order additional copies of this book, contact:
Xlibris
1-888-795-4274
www.Xlibris.com
Orders@Xlibris.com

Table of Contents

Foreword 9

A Book of Hope 11

Introduction 13

Note to all Parents, Teachers and other concerned Adults 15

Acknowledgements 17

Do you know about your Light? 19

The Power of Your Light 31

Our Deepest Fear Marianne Williamson, Author and Lecturer 43

How to Find your Light? 45

The Effect of your Light 51

Why your light may not Shine 55

    When your Light does not Shine 61

    Mindfulness and your Light 63

The Bully in Cyber Space and your Light 69

Your Relationships and Your Light 75

Your Parents, Your Family and Your Light 89

Do you know what you were born to do?

Foreword

For my brother from another mother, I have always admired you for your knowledge, wisdom, understanding, and most of all, for your sense of humor. You have always been able to make me laugh at the very funny things you say. Now, I am so proud of the work you did here with "Light Up Your Life." When you first told me the title and purpose of this book, it made me think about my own life as a teenager. As you know, my friends started a Rap group, "The Diplomats." They brought me into the group. But, being a rapper was not what I was born to do. I spent a lot of time in the group. I kept a low profile because I felt like I was not in a position to say much about how the group operated. Consequently, I did not reach my full potential because I was a part of somebody else's dream.

Although I am very grateful for the opportunity my friends gave me to join their rap group, and we will be friends for life, but now I am on my own path to fulfilling my purpose in life. It feels good to do what I do in the entertainment industry as a Reality TV Star, entertainer, rapper, soon to be author and perhaps even a movie star. Now, I am doing what I was born to do.

I am inspired by the work you did with this book. It has helped me to understand what it means to turn your light on, and I will use my gifts to influence change to make the world a better place. Thank you for the work you do with your books in the community, the education arena, and may you stay on the path to success in all that you do. Forever your boy, your cousin, and your brother from another mother.

Freekey Zeekey

A Book of Hope

For many of us, including myself, our lives can start off by things happening to us and around us that seem to make life so unfair. Especially since we are sometimes very young when we experience some of our worse life encounters. Early on, there are times we have bad experiences with people in our families who do things to us that may be unforgettable. Right now, you might already know what I am talking about based on some of your own early life experiences with family members or close family friends.

When bad things happen to us at a very young age, we may tend to lose hope because we have no idea if things can or will ever get better. Sometimes our view of the world and our personalities are shaped by what has happened to us. We might lose trust in people. We might feel insecure about some things. In addition, our willingness to communicate and feel good about ourselves can be diminished significantly. All because of the bad experiences we had with people we trusted.

Consequently, if we do not communicate about what happened to us, we cannot get any answers to the questions we may have about why these things happened, and how to solve those problems. Therefore, this Book of Hope was written to not only help us reconcile with the things that may have happened, but also to say that no matter what has happened, we can find happiness.

We were all born with a special talent. Our special talent comes to us by way of what is called, "This Little Light of Mine." One of the purposes of this book is to help us find out how to let our light shine. When we let our light shine, then we stop looking at our past. Instead, we start to look at ourselves. Then we take steps to recognize what we love to do. Hopefully, we will be inspired to turn our lights on and take steps to become what we were born to be.

The inspiration and motivation you generate when you realize the power of your light will launch you above your past experiences. No matter what may have happened in the past, it is important for you to "Keep hope alive," as the great Reverend Jesse Jackson use to say. In addition, you should always be encouraged. Things are never as bad as they seem. Right now, you hold the Book of Hope, which is designed to help you learn to win from the light you have within.

Introduction

How you doing? I hope all is well with you. Now that you have this book, consider this to be the end. When you finish, it will be the beginning of a new way of thinking and feeling about the way you live your life.

This book was inspired by the children I work with everyday during the travels of my social work journey. I meet children who look beautiful on the outside, and then I find out they are very sad on the inside. In many cases, I have found they are usually hurting because of mean things their schoolmates and other friends say about the way they look. Some of the children are chubby, some are skinny, some are gay, some are physically challenged in one way or another, and they are not considered perfect in the eyes of their peers. You should know, the truth of the matter is that nobody is perfect. When your schoolmates say bad things about you, that is because they are hurting too. They are not happy about the things that are not perfect in their lives, as well.

To make matters worse, the children I have met believe the negative words shouted at them by their schoolmates. I encourage these children to ignore the voices they hear from those who intend to hurt them. Instead, listen to the voice inside their own heads and send themselves a different message that says, "There is nothing wrong with me. I can do anything. All I have to do is try."

Then, I ask the children do they know about their light? They usually say, "What light?" I tell them we are all born with a special talent. There is a song that describes our special talent as coming to each and everyone of us by way of a little light. The light we are born with shines in different ways in which we can show the world our own special talent. The name of the song is, "This little light of mine." The children tell me they know that song. Some have said, "My grandmother sings that song to me." Other children have said, "I heard that song at my after-school program." I tell the children about the power of that song. I let the children know the words of that song say there is something very special about them. The song is so easy to sing, and they can make it their own. They can sing about their light. They can rap about their light, and they can talk about their light. I also let them know that my version of the song goes like this:

> This little light of mine, I"m gonna let it shine. Everywhere I go, I'm gonna let it shine, When I'm at work, I'm gonna let it shine. When I'm with my family, I'm gonna let it shine. When I'm by myself, I'm gonna let it shine, let it shine, let it shine...

I believe the amazing thing about this song is children of all ages and across all races know about this song. But, they have not made the song a part of their daily bread. By not doing that, I believe these children miss an opportunity to send themselves a message, on a daily basis, that would stimulate a positive feeling about themselves. That positive feeling could be the difference between an individual choosing to feel good and/or allowing others to make that individual feel bad.

For the record, This little light of mine, was written by Harry Dixon Loes around 1920 as a song for children. Although today it may be considered a gospel song, it also came to be an anthem of the civil rights movement in the 1950's and 60's.

For the purposes of this book, it is important to know, the key to a good life is to be aware of the power of the light inside of you. All good things work best from the inside out and that would include us as human beings. This book will show you the way to ignite your light so you can shine bright.

You were born with a special talent. It may be to sing, dance, write, draw, teach, preach, create, practice law, practice medicine, and/or play sports.

Whatever your special talent is, from this moment forward, you should strive to make your talent come alive-so you can do what you were born to do, and make the world a better place!

Note to all Parents, Teachers and other concerned Adults

Parents, first and foremost, please continue to encourage your children to get serious about their education. Today, it seems like some children do not connect with the idea that school enables them to develop skills they need to qualify for employment in the future. Please help your children see the connection between school and life as an adult. Hopefully, this will clarify why education is so important, and how it will empower them to eventually live on their own independent from you.

Also, now is the time for teachers and other concerned adults to take notice of children around them who demonstrate that their special talent is manifesting itself. For instance, when you see a child playing the piano well at five years old who has not taken any piano lessons, that is a sign that child's special talent is in full effect. Therefore, we as adults, no matter what our role is in the child's life, should start feeding into that individual's speical talent. If you are a parent, talk to the teachers to find resources to support the skill development of your child. If you are a teacher, talk to the parents about what you see in their children. Encourage parents to pursue programs to develop the special talents of their children.

Our children are just like the seeds we use to grow plants and flowers. They too, cannot grow and blossom into the talented children they are born to be unless we shed some light on them. We have to pay more attention to their individual talents so the children, their families, and society can reap from the harvest of their success.

What this will do for children is tremendous, but what this does for society is beyond measure. To discover a child's special talent, you can help that child fulfill their true purpose in life. You can help children avoid teen pregnancies. You can help children avoid drug use and gang affiliation. You can help children think about a college education. You can help children become productive members of society. You could also help to instill dreams in children that they might not normally envision because nobody ever helped them see their light.

Early on, children should be tuned into the ideas related to their special talents, or the importance of having a dream to fulfill their purpose in life.

If not, we may lose our children, as we already have in so many cases. Their skills go unnoticed. We feel like it is not our business to speak to their parents about what we see. Then, we lose our talented children to the devices of the street. From there, history tells us that the results are usually not positive.

Quite often, many of our children from all walks of life grow up and do not become what they were born to be. Many times, due to the lack of recognition by their own parents, children do not learn to turn their lights on. Therefore, if you are a parent, a grandparent, an aunt, an uncle, a teacher, a neighbor, a church member, or somebody from the community, pay attention to our children so they can begin to recognize themselves.

Another purpose of this book is to raise the awareness of all people with a targeted emphasis on our youth about the fact that we are all born with a special talent. As I said earlier, your special talent comes to you by way of what is called "This little light of mine." In order to find out what your special talent is, you have to pay more attention to yourself. When you look at yourself, you will begin to learn more about who you are and what you like to do.

Going forward, lets encourage our children to focus more on themselves. If we can get our children to turn on their lights, that will lead them to enjoy a life of happiness and self-actualization. Then we would have more fulfilled and successful children. When their lights are turned on, they are empowered to take control of their lives to create a brighter future for themselves. Thank you, and help to activate the light in the children near you…

Acknowledgements

I would like to recognize and acknowledge my good friend Dr. Kenneth B. Ballard for creating the exercises that are outlined throughout this book. The exercises will help you learn more about yourself from the inside out. The purpose of these exercises is to improve your Emotional Intelligence and initiate the process that will take the cover off of your light so it can shine bright. Thank you very much Dr. Ballard for providing these life changing instruments that raise awareness regarding the importance of Emotional Intelligence and facilitate healthy life experiences.

To my friend, KeiJuan Keitt, I would like to thank you for inspiring me to write this book. There is no question that your light is shining bright as an outstanding history teacher in the charter school system in Newark, New Jersey. Keep up the good work, and I believe only big things lie ahead for you in the future.

I would like to thank my father, Robet Thadd Gardner, Sr., for his full support in my efforts to complete this book. My father also encouraged me to complete this book despite any challenges that might come my way during the time it took me to complete this work. I would also like to mention that I admire how my father continues to live his life in a positive frame of mind despite the physical challenges that come with being 83 years old and counting.

Do you know about your Light?

Your light is the special talent that you were born with. Another way to define your light would be known as what some people say, "It is my calling" when they recognize they have a special talent. In other words, when a person realizes that they are naturally good at fixing cars, caring for animals, solving mathematical equations, carpentry, and fixing computers, these individuals know they have a special talent. In addition, your light gives you positive energy that you feel inside that causes you to be good to yourself and others.

On the other hand, there are people who do not know how to define their special talent. If that is you, please know there is a special talent inside of you too.

In this book, I will frequently refer to your special talent as your light. If you do not know about your light, I recommend that in order to activate your light, you simply have to make the choice that you will do something good with your life. Then, you must also learn how to feel good about yourself in order to keep your light shining bright. Now is the time to find out about your light. Now is the time to turn it on, and let it shine. With your light, you can make good things happen for you instead of letting bad things happen to you. Just like the sun rises everyday, so too should the light inside of you.

When your light is on, you will want to learn in school, and you will be on your best behavior. More importantly, when you feel good, it will allow you to exercise your creative will that is connected to the light inside of you. Guess what, there is nothing wrong with feeling good. It will help you to deal with tough times when you do not have lots of friends. When you feel good, it will give you confidence to know you can do anything, and believe all you have to do is try. The good thing about feeling good is that it feels good. It will help you to feel happy, and it does not cost any money for you to feel good.

When your light is on, you do not discriminate against people of color. You do not harbor any anti-semitic beliefs and behaviors. You do not espouse animus toward any members of the LGBTQ community. You would fully support diversity. Perhaps, you would even do some work to become culturally competent. You would assist people with disabilities, if necessary, in ways that highlight their abilities to get their jobs done at work. In fact, you would treat all people with dignity and respect. The light compels you to do what is right. Your light enables you to embrace any woman or man that people in society do not understand.

Throughout this book, I will constantly encourage you to turn your light on. Simply stated, what that really means is you just have to make a choice to create a better life for yourself. No matter what your present life circumstance is today, you can choose to make a better life for yourself. With that said, the choice to live a good life can be the key to finding out what you were born to be. As you think about what you want your life to be like, you may be inspired to figure out what you can do to make a better life for yourself.

I know that to be true. That is what I did to make a better life for myself. When I look at my life, as a child, after the deaths of my mother, my sister and my diagnosis with Type 1 Diabetes, I decided to make my life better. Then, as a teenager, I did the work to make it happen. You too can be that person who chooses the type of life you want to live.

Even though I say it is simply a choice you make to turn your light on, I do understand there may be some obstacles in your way. As you will come to learn in this book, your early family life experiences can sometimes seem like it may be impossible to find any happiness in this life. But, no matter what your life story is, you can turn your story into a source of inspiration to do what you were born to do. You see, we all have a story. I briefly shared my childhood story above, which I will discuss later in more detail.

The weird thing about life is that our story usually begins when we have our worse life experiences. It is your story that will either make you or break you. It is up to you to make it through those tough life experiences. Whenever your tough journey ends, your good life should begin.

To avoid the break up of your life, you must choose to wake up in your life. Use your story as inspiration to have a sense of purpose in your life. To do that, all you have to do is choose good over bad, glad over sad, right over wrong, and purpose over distress. Then, like I said before, make the choice to create a better life for yourself, which should flip the switch for your light to come on, and then you can "Light Up Your Life."

Think about this, it's no coincidence that when you come up with a good idea, you might refer to the idea as a "Bright" idea. Or, what about the fact that when we come to realize something that, at first, we did not understand, we tend to say, "Ah huh, a light came on, and now I understand what you were trying to say." It all starts with your light, your ideas, your dreams, your realization and your special talent.

When you turn your light on, you do not need a cell phone, twitter, snapchat, instagram, or extra data to make your light shine. As I already said, it is totally up to you to simply choose to make a better life for yourself. As a matter of fact, speaking of cell phones, are you a person who spends too much time locked in on your cell phone?

If you are locked in on your cell phone, then you are not focused on letting your light shine. How can you find out anything good about yourself if you spend all day looking at useless, non-essential images, and negative messages sent to you by somebody else? Instead of looking at your phone, look at yourself to figure out who you are. What do you know about yourself?

To answer that question, you will have to do something different on a daily basis. If I may suggest, put your cell phone to the side for a little while each day. Spend some quiet time with yourself. Take steps today so tomorrow will be better for you.

As long as you are staring at your cellphone all day, you do nothing to find any ways to feel good about yourself. To improve yourself, you have to look at yourself. How will you learn about your goodness if you are reading messages that send the wrong signals, looking at images that do not inspire good feelings, and be engaged in group chats about other group chats, which do not teach you how to solve your problems. In other words, the way you use your cellphone, right now, may be a waste of time.

Now, on the other hand, to get the most out of your cellphone, use it as a resource. Create your "Things to do" list by using the calendar on your phone to set dates and times for you to complete your daily responsibilities. The best way to get organized is to prioritize. You see, to shape your future, you have to plan your work. Then, work your plan. With your cellphone, not only can you plan your days, but also, you can find answers to all of your questions, as you already know, by utilizing Google. Stop playing. Start doing what you need to do in order to get where you want to go. Remember, whether you live a good life, or a bad life, that will be determined by the choices you make.

It is important to know that the key to being happy is to understand that happiness is a choice. Yes, you have to choose to be happy. It does not happen automatically. You have to do some work and tell yourself every day that you want to feel good. Choose to do things that make you feel good. Choose to think positive thoughts and do not think negative thoughts. Choose friends who think and behave in positive ways.

Now, lets get back to our discussion about your light. When you let your light shine, you will show respect for your parents, grandparents, teachers, schoolmates, police officers, and people who are different from you. When you feel good, you do not waste time thinking about how to start trouble.

Instead, you might participate in the science fair; you might compete in the national spelling bee; you could be the president of the student council; you could form a group to perform in a talent show; you could study to improve your grades; you could get involved in some community service, and most of all, you could have a dream about what you want to do when you grow up. Yes, it is also very important that you have a dream about what you want to do with your life. A dream about your future can give you a sense of purpose. A dream could be a source of inspiration for you.

In addition, your dream will help to keep you on track during times when you might be challenged by your peers to do things contrary to what is good for you. When your dream coincides with your special talent, it is only a matter of time before you will "Light up your life."

By now, you might ask, how do I find out what my special talent is? I would say that it may not always be easy. But, I would suggest that you start to pay close attention to yourself, and listen closely to what your family and friends say you do well. You might hear a relative say, "That boy is smart, he is going to be a doctor." My daughter is so talented. "She is going to be a superstar Broadcast Journalist." My nephew is so funny, "He could be the next great comedian."

It is important to note that your special talent will sometimes manifest itself at a very young age. Therefore, take some time to think about the things you really like to do. Think about things that seem to come natural and are easy for you to do.

For instance, I will tell you a story about when my special talent began to show. From the time I was in elementary school, in the third and fourth grades, I remember that I was the funniest person in the class. Most of the time, I intentionally said things to make my classmates laugh. Not only did I make my classmates laugh, but also I made my family and friends laugh all the time. When I look back at those times, my special talent clearly showed that I was very funny. Although I did not pursue comedy as my career choice, to this day, I still say things to make people laugh. I am still considered to be a very funny person amongst my family and friends.

As I stated above, I believe that comedy is my special talent. However, over the years I have excelled in a variety of areas using my other special talents as a human resources professional, as an author, a public speaker, and now in the field of social work. The moral of this story is that like me, you too may have been born with a variety of special talents.

Now, lets continue our discussion on the subject of how you can find your special talent. Some other things you can do is ask yourself questions that generate ideas about things you like to do. Think about the skills you have that come easy for you. Talk to people you admire about what they do. Google a variety of service organizations, healthcare organizations, branches of the military, and corporations to learn about their industries. You might even want to consider some entrepreneurial endeavors. The time is now for you to begin to realize your self-worth, and do things that will help you have lots of fun and enjoyment.

Make it your responsibility to find out what your special talent is, and you will live a good, abundant, and emotionally healthy life doing what you were born to do.

No matter who you are, what you look like, and how you self-identify from a gender perspective, whether you are short, tall, fat, skinny, black, white, yellow or brown and even if you are physically challenged, your light is there for you to let it shine. As it relates to your culture, no matter what it is, letting your light shine works for everyone.

There are some other things you should know about your light. When you let your light shine, you may lead and not follow your friends. You will find more positive things to do with your free time. The chances for you to succumb to alcohol and drug abuse would be diminished significantly.

As a young man, in high school, you would practice safe sex and not only avoid becoming a teenage father, but also avoid contracting a sexually transmitted disease (STD). You may find that gang banging is not for you. Instead, you may pursue a college education, and/or some entrepreneurial endeavors. You can be a positive force in your family, in your community and in your own way.

As a young woman, in high school, you would avoid fights with any girl who kissed your boyfriend, and you would understand that boy is not good for you. Instead, you may get involved in school social programs, explore career opportunities, go on college tours, avoid teen pregnancy, and avoid being infected by a sexually transmitted disease. You can be a positive force in your family, in your school, in your community, and in your own very special way.

The light is real. The light is yours. Turn it on. During your journey through the process of learning how to turn your light on, you will, on occasion, make some mistakes. You should know that as human beings, we all make mistakes. What is important is that you accept responsibility for your mistakes, and that you learn from your mistakes so you do not make the same mistakes again.

When you minimize your mistakes due to the lessons learned from the errors of your ways, your life will begin to move into a more positive space. Now you will be guided by the wisdom gained from your experiences, and this will also boost your confidence in your daily life activities. When your confidence is high, you have more courage to make good things happen in your life. You will see, things begin to go your way. When things go right, that is a sign of the power of your light.

Therefore, to stay on track with your positive energy, choose to fill dull periods of time with positive thoughts. Do not allow yourself to get bored. Instead, get busy. Please understand, no matter what your life is like today, that will not ruin your chances to live a good life tomorrow. Do not get stuck in the present. Look to your future. Do the work today in order to make your dream a reality tomorrow. Hold tight, as a child, teenager, or young adult, this is just the beginning of your life. You still have so much life to live. There is an old saying, "It does not matter how you start, what matters most is how you finish."

You might ask, why would I be born with a special talent? To that I would say, it is the natural order of things in the universe that you would be born with a special talent. Look around you. All of the clothes you have on today and everything you see: cars, planes, trains, ships, architecture, computers, cell phones, flat screen televisions, houses, swimming pools, and schools were created/invented by people just like you who had a special talent. All of these things go into making life good for you and society. Your special talent can lead to your happiness, success, and take you wherever you want to go in this life. Yes, why not you? "If you can see it, you can be it. Believe it, and you will achieve it!"

When you learn to feel good about yourself on a daily basis, your concern about yourself increases in positive ways, and improves your decision-making ability. Whereas, on the on the other hand, you can rest assure, when you do not feel good about yourself, you may tend to make careless and sometimes reckless decisions that can change the course of your life instantly. So please do not be afraid to prepare yourself for the good that is soon to come in your life. Deal with the issues that do not make you feel good about yourself. Those are the ones that you should talk about for resolution. Yes, talk about your issues in an effort to resolve those problems.

This chapter introduced you to your light, the good feelings you get from your light and ways to ignite the power of your light.

Therefore, to make sure you have the proper foundation to keep your light lit, it is important that you learn how to feel more secure about who you are.

To do that, I request that you go into the lab session below with an open mind, and start the work to become a better you. One way to do that is to improve your self-awareness. Learn more about yourself.

What do you know about yourself?

1. What do you like about yourself?

   _____

   _____

   _____

2. Do you know what makes you happy? Do you know what makes you mad?

   _____

   _____

   _____

3. What would you like to improve about yourself, and what steps will you take to make those improvements?

   _____

   _____

   _____

4. What do you know about your basic family tree (mother, father, grandparents) and where your family comes from?

   _____

   _____

   _____

5. Today, what do you believe is possible for you to achieve?

_____

_____

_____

6. Do you believe your destiny is predetermined, or do you believe your destiny can be determined by you?

_____

_____

_____

Do you have a dream?

Yes _____ / No _____

Why should you have a dream? A dream gives you vision towards your future. At some point in time, you will come of age where you will be expected by your parent(s), family members and peers to become more independent. Although, that time may be a long way off, your future is something you should be thinking about right now. After all, that is what this book is about. Finding out what your special talent is so you can do what you were born to do.

When you have a dream, it will provide you with some idea about what you want to do when you become an adult. Not only that, a dream will help you to see your way out of difficult situations you might be experiencing during your childhood years. For instance, while growing up in Harlem, I was surrounded by poverty, drug addiction, gang violence, and a community dependent on public assistance. However, what really helped me is that I always saw my way out of my neighborhood no matter what I experienced along the way. I had a dream of a better life for myself.

Therefore, please know that a dream is the key to seeing where you could be. If you can see it, you can be it. All you have to do is take the steps to follow the path that will lead you to realize your dream.

Dreams do come true. By mere virtue of the fact that you are reading this book, and changing your life for the better has made my dream come true.

In addition, a dream provides you with a better focus to keep your life on track. When you aspire to fulfill your dream, you improve your chances to stay out of trouble. You move yourself above things like being a teenage parent, being a gang member, dropping out of high school, drug abuse, and any other major distraction during your teenage years that could derail your life if you have no vision.

How to find a dream about your future? You can use your imagination. Close your eyes and meditate every day on what you want to do that would make you happy. Think about what you want to do that could help you earn a lot of money. Think about all of the good things you can do that would make other people happy, and make the world a better place.

Then, think about where you want to live when you do what you dreamed about. Use your phone to Google career choices that peak your interest. Talk to adults you know about what they did to reach their goals.

The more you talk to people, the more you will learn. Then, you just might start to "Dream the impossible dream."

Will you start to dream about your future now?

Yes_____/ No_____

The Power of Your Light

Now that you know about your light, let's talk about how bright your light is right now. Just for clarification and relevance, when we look for light bulbs, we look to see how bright the bulbs are in terms of their "Wattage," which is noted on the bulbs. In other words, the higher the wattage, the brighter the light bulb. As you know, a 100 watt bulb is brighter than a 20 watt bulb. Since we are talking about your light, I use the light bulb example here as a symbol of the light inside of you. Therefore, when I ask above, how bright is your light right now? I am really asking do you know anything about your special talent and are you feeling good about yourself right now? Therefore, if you believe your light is on at the present time, what would you say to the question below?

How bright is your light?

20 Watts____   40 Watts____   60 Watts_____   80 Watts or brighter_____

Is there anything about you that shows your light is on?

_____

_____

If your light is not bright (20 – 60 Watts), what will you do to make your light brighter? (80 – 100 Watts)

_____

_____

If your light is not on, why have you not turned your light on?

_____

_____

_____

_____

Before we go further in our discussion about the power of your light, you first have to understand that there should be no circumstance, no issue, no problem, and no excuses that prevent you from activating the power of your light. In other words, I encourage you to believe that nothing can stop you, other than yourself. The power of your light can help you overcome any situation. In order to give yourself a chance, always be encouraged. Do not be discouraged.

If you believe that you are currently living in a difficult situation at home or otherwise, which may create a challenge for you to turn on the power of your light, history shows us that you are not alone. There is always somebody else who is going through some difficult times like you. In many cases, you would be surprised to find out that their story may be ten times worse than yours. Somehow, they rose above their circumstance to live a good life.

You should know, the worse things that happen to you can also inspire you to become a change agent for a good cause. That means you do work to create solutions to make life better for yourself and others regarding your respective issue. You can turn tragic, sad, and bad times into glad, happy and joyful times when you realize the power you have within.

Now, lets talk about the history that shows you are not alone:

I want to share my childhood story. Just like you may have experienced, I also had no control over what happened to me, and I had no idea these things would happen.

Once upon a time, when I was nine years old, I went outside to play all day. It was a typical day for me as a child. When I came home later that evening, my family was gathered at my house because my mother collapsed. She had a brain aneurism, which means she was bleeding in her head. My mother was rushed to the hospital by ambulance.

She was unconscious for the rest of the night. The next day, my mother died. Just like that, my mother was gone forever. Shocked, broken hearted and bewildered, I cried until I could not cry anymore.

Afterwards, for a long period of time, it was very difficult for me. I cried a lot thinking about my mother and how much I missed her. Yet, at the same time, I did not stop moving forward with my life. It was really tough when I heard music on the radio that she use to play in the house while she cleaned up. As funny as this may sound, crying a lot was actually good for me. It helped me release the sorrow I felt for the loss of my mother. Also, I talked to my family and friends about how much I missed my mother and that helped me too. Talking really helped me to release most of the bad feelings I felt at that time. Fortunately, for me, I came from a very supportive family. I also had lots of friends to keep me busy playing the fun games we played at that time.

Prior to my mother's death, it all started for me where I grew up in Harlem USA. I lived in a public housing development, aka, the projects. As a child, I had to fight bullies in order to play in the parks. I lived in a neighborhood ravished by poverty, crime, and over-crowded with heroin addicts. On a regular basis, with my friends, I had to stand up to their peer pressure. I had to choose high school over drug use. I chose to stay in school and not drop out of high school with the rest of the crowd. I used condoms to avoid becoming a teenage father. I chose not to smoke cigarettes even though that was considered the coolest thing to do. I believe my light was on (60-65) watts, but I did not realize the actual power of my light. However, the little bit of light I had helped me because I did not care what my friends thought about me. I did not follow them when they chose to make foolish decisions.

While I was working my way through all of this as a child, three years after my mother past away, my oldest sister died from an overdose of heroin. She was only 20 years old. By the time I was 12 years old, both my mother and my sister were dead. Just as I was finding ways to cope with the loss of my mother and my sister, three years later, I became very sick. I was diagnosed with "Type 1" diabetes at the age of 15. I too was rushed to the hospital. The doctors informed my family that if they had waited 15 more minutes before they brought me to the hospital they would have been picking out a coffin for me.

During the time I was hospitalized, I was devastated when a nurse informed me that I would have to take insulin by injection for the rest of my life. I will never forget, the nurse walked into my room. She threw a syringe and a vial of insulin on my hospital bed. I asked her, "What are you doing, this is your job? You are supposed to give me this needle." I thought the nurse just had to give me some medicine since I was in the hospital.

The nurse said, "Oh no sugar, you have to learn how to do this so you can take care of yourself after you leave the hospital. You are a diabetic, and this is how you will survive from now on." It was like "Boom," I was totally mortified! Just like when my mother died, I cried until I could not cry anymore.

After that traumatic experience, the doctors at Mount Sinai Hospital gave me a book to read. I read that book. This book taught me how to live with diabetes. The book also taught me to understand that if I manage my diabetes, I could live a normal healthy life, as a diabetic. I was inspired to do just that. I told myself that I would control my blood sugars. I made a promise to myself that I would not die because of diabetes.

It was easy for me to make that promise to myself. I learned a lot about how my life would be as a diabetic from the book I read. Also, at the time I was diagnosed with diabetes, my doctors explained to me that if I did not manage my diabetes properly, I could experience a lot of complications with my health. I was told that I could go blind, I could experience kidney failure, and numbness in my feet that could lead to the amputations of my legs. Those are just a few of the things that could have happened to me if I did not manage my diabetes.

Meanwhile, during my recovery in the hospital, I was inspired by my diagnosis with diabetes to take a good look at my future. That is when I decided to turn my light all the way up and let it shine. Remember, I was 15 years old at the time. I decided that I would finish high school, and go to college. I declared that I would make a success out of my life. As bad as things were for me at the time, with my mother dying suddenly, with my sister overdosing on heroin, and then I was diagnosed with diabetes, I was inspired to overcome the tragedies in my life. That inspiration motivated me to rise above my life circumstances and become a success despite the odds. I was actually inspired during the most difficult three year period of time in my life.

As it has turned out, not only did I get a college degree, but also I have two master's degrees. I have been successful in corporate America as a Human Resources professional. I have started two businesses, I am happily married with three children, I have authored three self-help relationship books, which includes this book. Most of all, despite the early tragic deaths of my mother and sister, I am very happy today. My mother would have wanted me to move on with my life and make something out of myself. I believe those experiences made me a stronger and better person. I am so glad that I let my light shine during the most difficult challenges of my life.

Although this is my story, I guarantee you if there is somebody you admire, whether they are famous or not, research their life story, and you will find that they too have had to overcome tremendous obstacles to be what they are today.

The moral of my story is that there is nothing special about me. Yet, I was able to overcome the devastating experiences of my childhood. If I could do it, then so can you.

Therefore, what you should learn from my story is that tragedy can strike at any time. Yes, our loved one's lives could end suddenly. Family members and friends get sick with illnesses that lead to death. Sometimes we make bad choices that cause fatal outcomes. Tomorrow is not promised to you. In fact, the next moment in a day is not promised to you. When you experience trials and tribulations, not only do you need your light to shine, but also you need to be resilient (have inner-strength) so you can handle most anything that might come your way. The funny thing is, in life, some of us are more resilient than others. Just like some people are tall and some people are not. Somehow, resilience just seems to work that way in different people. There are some who are innately resilient, and have natural inner-strength to handle some of life's most difficult experiences.

However, for those of you who may not be as resilient as others, there is something else I would like to tell you about that can help you to become resilient. I would like to introduce you to my favorite subject. The subject is called Emotional Intelligence. This is another source of inner-strength you have and you can use to regulate your emotions.

You might ask, what is Emotional Intelligence? Unlike resilience, which as previously stated is a natural inner-strength some people have to find resolve to handle the ups and downs of everyday life. Emotional Intelligence can be learned and used to strengthen your resolve to handle the highs and lows of everyday life that you will experience. Your next question might be, how do I learn more about my Emotional Intelligence? I would say, that is a good question, and the answer to your question lies below on the pages that follow. There you will find a step by step process to start you on your journey to improve your Emotional Intelligence.

Life should be filled with joy all the time. However, for all people, pain and some suffering is a part of our lives as human beings. What we should know is that it is not what happens to us in life that matters, instead it is how we respond to what happens to us that really matters. If you come through your painful life experiences in a healthy positive way, you can "Turn your pain into gain."

Keep in mind, sometimes life will be tough. When you go through tough times, try to do things to "Turn lemons into lemonade." In order to do that, you have to take control of yourself. Then, take control of your life. What I say about the power of your light is true if you let it shine. Just try it. I dare you. The key to all of this is that you have to want it in order to create a better life for yourself. If you do, then you simply decide to make a better life for yourself.

This chapter focused on the need to be resilient because some very unfortunate things can happen suddenly during your life experience, which can affect the power of your light if you let it. Consequently, some of those life experiences might seem hard to overcome. In addition, those life experiences are even harder to overcome if you are unable to move beyond the pain, the memory, and the emotional mindset that you have sustained for a particular hardship experience. To assist you with navigating through the process of getting pass these experiences, we believe you should take some steps to improve your Emotional Intelligence.

How to Improve your Emotional Intelligence?

Please give careful consideration to the questions outlined below. You will be asked to answer some tough questions about your life experiences. In addition, you will be asked to take an assessment of your life regarding past experiences and any traumatic life events. Please note, not only is Emotional Intelligence a way to improve your resilience, but also good Emotional Intelligence will help you to overcome your unresolved personal childhood issues, which may interfere with your ability to feel good and be good to others. In other words, it is very important for you to understand the connection between your childhood experiences and your adult life. In many ways, the way you feel and behave today is directly related to the life experiences you had as a child.

For instance, I have met boys and girls who do not know their fathers. As teenagers and young adults, they have expressed their anger and resentment about the fact that they do not know their fathers. This has caused them to be angry, sometimes depressed, and feeling unwanted. The fatherless experience also causes these individuals to feel insecure, lack trust for people and have low self-esteem. Therefore, when you start to recognize what may be causing you to behave in certain ways, then you can take steps to learn how to let go and forgive family members and others who may have hurt you in the past. This is another way to start the process to turn on your light.

If you do not address your issues now, you will revisit your issues later. In other words, when you do not resolve your childhood personal issues as a young person, you will bring those issues into your adult relationships. However, by then, you may have to assess even more damage in your life related to bad decisions you made because you did not improve your Emotional Intelligence. Therefore, lets move on to the lab session below, and start the work to improve your Emotional Intelligence.

Make a list of your experiences that have caused issues for you, i.e., traumas, relationships, family issues and other major life experiences.

_____

_____

_____

Can you identify the past experiences that are currently hindering your ability to feel good about yourself today?

_____

_____

_____

Which experiences continue to bother you, and what steps will you take to resolve those issues? If I may suggest, start talking to someone about those experiences to find some relief.

_____

_____

_____

List the effect of your unresolved issues in your relationships with yourself, family members and others.

_____

_____

_____

Now that you have identified the unresolved issues in your life, list some ways you plan to be open in communication, true to yourself and others so you can work to resolve your issues.

_____

_____

_____

Share your thoughts below on any other issues that may concern you. Talk about what you can do to improve your Emotional Intelligence in regards to those issues. The more you talk, the better you will feel.

_____

_____

_____

So, how was that experience? Can you feel it? Are you starting feel any better? If not, please understand that sometimes when we look back at things that hurt us the most, we may not feel good right away.

But, if you talk about it enough, try to forgive and let go, you will feel the positive vibe you get when you try to resolve your issues the right way. Keep working: this is a process.

Okay, before we leave this chapter, lets look at what a renown author and lecturer, Marianne Williamson, has to say about your light. See her powerful quote on page 43.

I share this quote with you to show that the subject of your light is bigger than me. There are so many others who understand the power of your light.

We are all born with a special talent.

Our Deepest Fear
Marianne Williamson, Author and Lecturer

It is our light not our darkness that frightens us
"Our deepest fear is not that we are inadequate. Our deepest fear is that we are powerful beyond measure. It is our light not our darkness that most frightens us. We ask ourselves, who am I to be brilliant, gorgeous, talented and fabulous? Actually, who are you not to be? You are a child of God Your playing small does not serve the world There's nothing enlightened about shrinking so that other people won't feel insecure around you. We were born to make manifest the glory of God that is within us. It's not just in some of us; it's in everyone. And as we let our own light shine, we unconsciously give other people permission to do the same. As we are liberated from our own fear, our presence automatically liberates others."

I would like to thank Marianne Williamson for granting me permission to share this powerful quote with you. Ms. Williamson is the author of 11 books including four of which were on the New York Times Best Sellers List. A special note about her first book, A Return to Love (1992), which has sold in excess of three million copies, and is one of the first books to be endorsed by Oprah Winfrey.

How to Find your Light?

First and foremost, as previously stated in chapter one, it is important for you to pay more attention to yourself. Take some time to spend time with yourself. While you are by yourself, start to think about things you really like to do. Think about the things you have accomplished, and what you enjoyed about the work that led to those accomplishments. Ask yourself this question, do you really know who you are? You owe it to yourself to find out who you are, and what motivates you to do more.

Sometimes, we take ourselves for granted. We pay more attention to other people than we do to ourselves. The thought of what you like to do may get lost while you are looking at somebody else. Now is the time to start thinking about you, and not only what you like to do, but also what you love to do.

From this moment forward, stop looking for love in other places like a boy/girlfriend, a baby, a new cell phone, and what other people have. Instead, look no further than yourself. Everything you could ever want and/or need is already within your grasp. All you have to do is recognize that you are more than enough.

You may not find out what you love to do in one day. But, if you start looking, you may find out what you love to do more sooner than later. When you discover what you enjoy doing, you begin to tap into the process of turning your light on.

If you get bogged down in your thoughts, and cannot find answers to the question of what you like to do right away, talk to people who know you. Listen to what they say about you. Perhaps, they may be able to offer suggestions about how they see you, and what they discovered about your special talent(s). Remember, this is a process, which means that it may take some time for things to come into view for you. So, stick to it until you are able to turn your light on. You will know when your light is on because it feels good. Whatever your special talent is, it will begin to reveal itself to you.

On the other hand, if your journey to find your special talent is not as easy as it relates to what is described above, that might be due to the fact that you may have grown up under some very challenging circumstances. Most of which were beyond your control. As I described above, many things about your emotional state of mind as a young person or as an adult, stems from experiences you had in your childhood. In other words, good childhood experiences usually allow people to feel good when they grow up. Bad and/or traumatic childhood experiences may cause a variety of personal issues related to poor communication skills, low self-image, bitterness, loneliness, and even depression during your teenage and adult life. If these types of issues are not resolved early in your life, they will come with you to your friendships, your relationships and most of all, the relationship you have with yourself. It may be hard for you to find ways to be happy with yourself.

Therefore, you may have to look back over your life experiences, as you did at the end of chapter two. If you were subjected to traumatic experiences related to domestic violence between your parents, or if you were the victim of either physical or sexual abuse at the hands of one of your family members, or somebody else, then as a young person, it might take a lot of courage for you to face your unresolved childhood issues. That would be as a result of the pain you may still feel when you revisit your memories of those events. Please know that you are not alone, and I hope you can find the strength to reconcile with these issues so you can get to the feel good part of your life. We all have unresolved childhood issues. One of the best ways to get over your issues is try to deal with them head on. Remember, the goal is to get pass the pain to find the joy.

Try to work through your tough life experiences. Talk about the experiences with somebody close to you. Remember, it is best to talk about what bothers you. If not, you will act out about what troubles you. Usually, the outcomes of that behavior will lead to negative consequences.

In some cases, you may not find closure to your most troubling issues. The people who have caused your pain may be in a different place today. Or, they simply may not acknowledge you in connection with those past experiences. Therefore, you have to learn how to let go of bad experiences with bad people. By letting go of your past, that will free you to enjoy your future. You will improve your chances to let your light shine.

In addition, another step in your healing process would be to learn more about the history of the person who violated you. This is very important because more than likely you will learn that whoever violated you, they too probably were violated in the same way by a family member or a close family friend. Be advised, parents parent the way they were parented. In other words, if your father physically or sexually abused you, more than likely his father did the same thing to him.

That is why it is important to learn about the history of the person who violated you. Because as much as it is there fault for what they did to you, at least, it might help you to understand why they violated you in such a terrible way. To have a better understanding of the big picture, is always helpful in the letting go and forgiving process.

To let go and forgive is a good method to use in order for you to move forward and live your life. Live the life that is intended for you by removing the issues that take the shine off of your light. Your light cannot shine when it is blocked by unresolved issues from your past.

Therefore, another important step in the process is that you must first acknowledge that you have some issues before you can take steps to resolve those problems. Then, you would be better able to go forward into your future with more joy and happiness.

If you find it hard to look back at what you consider to be doom and gloom of your past, perhaps you should change the way you look at things. Look at it as your journey to zoom in order to bloom so you can blossom into the person you were born to be. After all, if you were violated in any way, then you have already experienced the doom and gloom. Now, it is time to break through and become unstuck from your past.

The next lab session is the one that will help you make room in your life for all the good that is to come your way. This is where you can learn how to let go of bad memories of bad experiences with bad people. Now is the time to turn the page on yesterday, and look forward to tomorrow and the rest of your life…

Learn to   Let go

Working through issues from your past is vital to forming healthy feelings about yourself, your current and future relationships. Do you find yourself thinking about past experiences that may not have been your best times? If so, you may not have allowed yourself to experience closure. When you do not get proper closure, you may carry bad emotions with you everywhere you go.

It is important for you to realize that closure begins and ends with you. You may not always be able to rely on the person who wronged you to either acknowledge or apologize for the pain they brought into your life. You probably will not get an explanation regarding their action as to why they did what they did to you.

Therefore, whether or not you get the answers, you must learn to free yourself from memories that contribute to your unhappiness regarding your past experiences. You simply have to let go! For example, if you drop a glass, it will break. You sweep up the broken glass. You throw it away, and you get another glass.

Below are five questions listed to assist you with the process of working through the challenges related to letting go of bad experiences from your past. This may not be something that will happen overnight.

It is a process that will require you to come to terms with the fact that those experiences, and/or relationships have ended. As shrewd as it may sound, the reality is you just have to let go, and move on with your life.

1. What prevents you from finding closure regarding your past experiences?

   _____
   _____
   _____

2. Can you overcome those issues?

   _____
   _____
   _____

3. What steps will you take to make sure you work through the issues from your past to bring positive closure to those issues?

   _____
   _____
   _____

4. What lessons have you learned from your previous experiences?

   _____
   _____
   _____

5. Can you list some reasons why it would be important for you to let go of memories of bad experiences with bad people?

   _____
   _____
   _____

Learning to let go is hard to do. However, when you allow yourself to let go and look forward, you will allow yourself to experience the joy of what lies ahead in your future. If you do the math, it is quite simple. You have two options. One, you can remain stuck in the past with memories of what causes you pain and holds you back.

Or two, you can stop looking back at what happened in the past. You will not be able to change anything about what happened during that time. I do not say this to make light of any traumatic experiences you have endured. That is not what I am trying to do. Instead, I want you to stop hurting about your past, and move on with your life. Give yourself a chance to make tomorrow better than yesterday!

The Effect of your Light

So far, I have talked a lot about your light, and what you have to do to let it shine. I have also talked about the reasons why it is so important that you find your light. You should not live your life without realizing who you really are and what you were born to do. That would mean the world did not shine as bright because you did not shine your light.

As you know, your light is your own special talent you can use to light up your life. When your life is lit, there is a movement of energy that goes on inside of you. This energy compels you to move in a way that you want to do more to let your light shine every where you go.

When your light is shining, you will stand out in a crowd. Everyone knows when somebody is shining in the group. The group can feel the energy generated by your light.

In addition, the effect of letting your light shine can help you solve problems more effectively. In other words, you will feel more confident, and you will be better able to handle problems as they arise. Please take note of this, you should not let your problems be the focus. Instead, if you have a problem, focus on the solution that will solve that problem. Do not get stuck in the problem. Problems do not have to last long. The faster you solve your problems, the sooner you can get back to the good times. It is your choice to either strive for happiness, or try to survive in your choice to remain in a state of sadness.

The effect of your light may help you understand that you should choose to be happy. It will guide you to make good choices by using consequential thinking. In other words, see the outcome of your decisions before you decide.

Listen up, if you did not think about this before, you should think about it now. You only live once. Tomorrow is not promised to you, and tomorrow is not promised to anybody you love. Therefore, try to live each day to the fullest. In other words, have fun. Create opportunities for yourself. Save your money. Volunteer to help somewhere. Boys respect the girls. Girls respect the boys. Men respect the women. Women respect the men. Learn to love yourself. Learn to let go of bad experiences. Learn to forgive. Apologize for something you did wrong. Forgive yourself for mistakes you have made. Say hello to a schoolmate that you do not know. Say hello to somebody you do not know in your community. Try something new. Set yourself a part from the crowd. Show respect for your parents, elders, teachers, and yourself.

The effect of your light helps you to feel more secure. You do not envy others. You realize that jealousy is a total waste of time. Think about this, why should you worry about a boy or girl (man or woman) who does not want to be with you. Let them go. Your next relationship will give you a chance to find the person who may want to be with you.

If you are the jealous type, think about this. You cause yourself lots of stress. Stress does not make you feel good. You also cause lots of stress for the other person. Stress is not good for your health. It makes you feel anxious. Stress makes you feel nervous. Stress can make you feel confused. Most of all, stress can make you feel unhappy because you are jealous, and you do not trust your boyfriend or your girlfriend. Therefore, learn to focus on yourself. You should be what is most important in your life. Learn to love yourself first. Then, it will be easier for you to love another person without stress or the strife that, as a jealous person, you would bring to their life.

To love without jealous stress, brings you and yours more happiness. You should choose happiness over stress.

In addition, you can avoid more stress if you stop using your cellphones to record fights between your friends and other schoolmates. You may think you are having fun by watching your friends brutally beat one another. But, what you are really doing is recording the evidence that police will use to arrest you, and prosecutors will use to convict you for felony assault(s).

Intelligent people do not record the evidence that can be used against them in a court of law. Think about this, you take part in a crime. Then, you record what you and your friends did to break the law. When the police arrest you, they will take your phone. Then, the police will have all of the evidence necessary to prove you took part in a crime.

You can turn stress into a positive experience. If you must stress, then stress to do better on your next test. Stress to complete your college applications. Stress the need to achieve success in whatever you do. Stress and strive to be a better person.

The effect of your light will help you to live in the positive. You will choose education over incarceration. You will choose participation over childhood emancipation. Recognize your power and the effect of your light.

Some of the main ideas of this chapter stress the importance of what you can do to become a better person. Also, we discussed that you should learn to feel more secure about who you are. This would be required to stimulate the power of your light. With that said, in the lab session below, there are two questions you can review that will give you some food for thought on how to become more self-assured and feel more secure. In addition, there are some tips I provided to show you how easy it is to feel more secure.

Learn to feel more secure

Why should you learn to feel more secure? First, your light will not shine if you are insecure. Secondly, when you feel secure, it will make you more comfortable with yourself, and in your dealings with people regarding life's daily challenges. It is important to feel comfortable with yourself. We are not talking comfort in a relaxing way. But, comfort in a way of having confidence in that whether you are short, tall, skinny or fat, white or black, have long hair, short hair, or no hair at all, you have developed a liking for yourself whereby you feel totally good about you.

The good feeling that comes with being more secure will give you courage to take risks to try positive things. More importantly, when you feel more secure, that will effectuate the power of your light. You shine in all that you do. You will conduct yourself in a way that enhances your swag. When your swag is up, your positive vibe will spread to everything you do.

 ## How to feel more secure?

1. Learn to focus exclusively on yourself. Do not compare yourself to others. You have to apply a mindfulness way of thinking about yourself. That means that you should stay in tuned to yourself one thought at a time.

2. Do not worry about things like what your boyfriend/girlfriend is doing with other people. You cannot control what they do anyway.

3. Think less about what you do not have, and appreciate what you do have.

4. Focus on your strengths, which are the things that you are good at doing.

5. Do not make room in your mind for negative thoughts, memories, and/or other things that do not make you feel good about yourself.

6. Remember, this is a process. To feel more secure may not happen overnight. But, it will happen when you focus on the good and not the bad.

Why your light may not Shine

In the previous chapters, I briefly discussed some of the reasons that may not allow your light to shine. In this chapter, I will talk in more detail about those reasons and/or life experiences that may not let your light shine.

You might wonder why I have talked so much about the dark side of life. The reason for that is because the dark issues are real. These issues affect all people. If not you, then I bet you know somebody who has lived in the dark before they saw their light.

What is most important here is that, as I have said before, when you recognize the dark side of your life, that is how you get to the bright side of your life. Ironically, to get to the good, you have to go through the bad. This is what I mean when I say we all have a story. Sometimes, the bad experiences we have is where our story begins. When our story ends, is where our light begins...

So, let me be very clear. This book is not about the dark. This book is about the light. I talk about the dark because in order to get to the light we have to come out of the dark.

Now, in so many ways, the reasons why your light may not shine could be a difficult question to answer. There are a myriad of factors that come into play that may lead to the reason(s) why your light may not shine. However, everything about us as human beings starts with our families of origin. We are all born into some type of family situation whether you have a mother and father in your household, adopted parents, foster parents, grandparents, aunt and uncle, a bio parent and step parent, interracial parents, or two parents of the same sex. Your personal experience as to how you are cared for by your caretakers, and what you observe in their behavior during your childhood determines in many cases why your light may not shine.

First of all, parents may not focus on your light. There are many other concerns for families when it comes to children. Financial reasons, bad relationships, drugs, alcohol, poverty, divorce, sickness, and death are all part of family life that take the focus off of your light. The light is not a regular subject of general discussion in families, with friends, in school, with doctors, in sports, television/radio programs, and in many cases, not in our churches' either.

At this point, it is probably safe to say that when it comes to finding out about who you are and what you were born to do, as it relates to your light, it is not really discussed in our family settings. That is not to say that is a bad thing. I think, in many cases, our families may not even think about the light. You cannot see it. You cannot touch it. The light is not for sale at the malls. In addition, the subject of your light basically is a non-factor because of all of the issues noted above. I am willing to bet, until now, for many of you, this is the first time you have learned about both the significance and the importance of that light of yours.

My hope is that by the time you finish reading this book that you tell your parents about the light inside of you. I hope you tell them that you will find your special talent so you know what you were born to do. And, please tell them that you know something about their light too.

Now, lets take a look at some other family dynamics that may get in the way of your calling to do what you were born to do.

For instance, you are born into a family that is wealthy. In that case, there may not be a focus on your light because there is usually a path and pressure from your parents to be like them to follow their road to success.

You want to be a musician, and that is not good enough for your parents. Or, you are the first male born in your household, and your father has chosen you to run his business, take over his church, or be a doctor just like him. In those cases, your light may not receive any consideration from your parents because, in their minds, their way is the best way for you to succeed.

In another case, your mother may be a famous dancer, school administrator, entrepreneur, and you may want to play professional basketball as a woman in the WNBA. However, your dreams are not acceptable to your mother. It can be a difficult situation when you figure out what you love to do, and your parent(s) do not support your dreams.

In other family scenarios, it can be far worse. Some of us are born into families where we see domestic violence between our parents. The constant and persistent extreme levels of violence will definitely affect our view of the world, how we deal with our relationships, and may overshadow the power of our light. Some of us grow up in households where our parents abuse alcohol and drugs. When our parents abuse these substances, we may experience a poor quality of life. There will be no focus on our light coming from our parents.

Then, there are situations where some of you may have been physically abused by a parent. For others, you may have been sexually abused by a parent, an uncle, an aunt, a neighbor, friends and other people close to your family. These experiences will most definitely dim the power of your light and stifle your progress toward a positive view of the world. In cases of sexual and physical abuse, along with the length of time you may have experienced those traumatic encounters, you will definitely be presented with a huge and complicated challenge trying to find the power of your light.

Due to the fact that each of these cases takes on its own horrific experience in the eyes of the victims, none of these experiences are the same for anybody who has had to endure such violations of their childhood.

It is always important to talk about what is heavy on your heart. When you hold on to painful experiences by not talking about them, then for sure you will act out in ways that are not true to who you really are. In cases where you cannot work through these difficult emotions on your own, you should seek to work with a counselor. If you are not very resilient, in these cases, your light may never shine.

These type of traumatic life experiences can have a devastating affect on your life overall. Victims of these types of abuses tend to be depressed, experience suicidal ideations, act out in school, abuse drugs, alcohol, have low self-esteem, and have a total lack of trust of people in general. In addition, your adult relationships will more than likely be dysfunctional in that when you have experienced turbulence, violence, and confusion in your childhood, that may become your model for future relationships. Then you may abuse your children and/or your intimate partner.

If your issues related to these experiences are not resolved, then your adult behavior may resemble the same abusive behavior you experienced as a child. As I have said before, we tend to parent the way we were parented. Without proper attention to these issues, then you may perpetuate the behavior you learned from your family members when you were a child.

In other words, it is very possible you will deal with your children the same way your parents dealt with you. Then, the light of your children may not shine and then your children's children light may not shine. This can go on for generations to come in your family.

What you should know is that we all have some type of unresolved issues that we experienced from our childhood. As my wife always says, "It is important for you to know that what happened to you when you were a child is not your fault. However, as an adult, it is your responsibility to address the issues that may affect your ability to feel good about yourself." If not, as previously noted, you may experience a lot of emotional pain because of your unresolved issues. Deal with your past, so you can turn on your light and enjoy your future.

Aside from the issues stated above regarding the life experiences that may not allow your light to shine, for some individuals, they may have other challenges which are related to their sexual orientation that may dim their light. Please note, if that is you, I do not believe your light may not shine because you may have questions related to your sexual orientation. What I am saying is that challenges may arise with your family and friends because they may not understand your behavior as it relates to your wavering sexual orientation. The discomfort, for you, caused by the pressure that could arise from the tension generated by that issue could dim your light.

You see, the reality is that in many situations, it may be hard for family and some friends to understand that some boys do not always feel like boys. And, why their behavior as to their mannerisms seem to come across as being more feminine than masculine. Whereas the same thing is true for females in that some families do not understand why there are some girls who do not always feel like girls, and their mannerisms manifest themselves as being more masculine than feminine.

This may not only be very confusing for the individuals who experience these feelings, but also it may be confusing, and in some ways, very disappointing to your parents who may apply pressure on you to be more like what they want regarding your sexual orientation. This stress may affect your ability to turn your light on.

The tension, the criticism, the confusion, the isolation, the shame, the embarrassment, and the fact that you cannot control how you feel can make it very difficult to work through the family strife to find that light of yours. Although, today, unlike many years ago, there has been great progress made in society overall regarding acceptance of members of the LGBTQ community.

However, in many of our families, there is little, if any, understanding of a boy who presents like a girl, and a girl who presents herself like a boy.

Our parents want boys to be boys, and girls to be girls. This can be a painful struggle for you, as a young person. Your family members, in many cases, believe you are making a choice to act in ways that are different from your biological gender. In those cases, the idea of your light trying to shine may be totally diminished.

Whereas, in your mind, if you were allowed to be who you really are, then the path to your light would be easier to travel. In other words, to be accepted by your family as you are, would make your life so much easier. That would empower you to accept your own differences without shame and embarrassment.

Nevertheless, what you should embrace is that you are who you are. You cannot be who your parents want you to be, or what they do not want you to be when it comes to your sexual orientation.

Now, as time goes by, your parents may not want you to live in their house while you experience these changes in your feelings, and in your thoughts about your sexual orientation. Therefore, you know who you are. You have no choice. You have to turn on your light, and do the work to progress your life in a way that you will not have to depend on your parents. This is a hump you may have to jump over by yourself.

With all due respect to your parents, your family and friends who may not accept you for who you really are, in order for you to be free, you must be you. Hopefully, in time, your loved ones will come to appreciate you in your successful life, in your joy and your happiness as a gay person who let their light shine just like everybody else. You do have a light. Let it shine.

For the good people who society says, because of your lifestyle whatever it may be, you are outside the box of what is considered normal and/or acceptable in the eyes of the society police, you too were born with a special talent.

Although you may be heavily burdened with pain, pressure and persecution for being who you feel you are supposed to be, unfortunately we live in a world that is not accepting of all people who may not fit the limited mold of what is considered to be "Normal."

Yet, you are here for a reason. You may be struggling and striving to push the agenda for your life without any support from those who loved you before you discovered your true identity. I proclaim you too were born with a light that gives you a special talent.

But, you must first realize that the journey to your light may be more difficult due to the harsh realities of mean spirited people in and around your life. Whereby, they may try to stifle your walk on your journey. If so, your journey has to be defined by your will to live. Your will to give yourself a chance to be independent from those who are not for you. You must do things that not only empower you, but also you should seek people and organizations who support you. That way, you will be in a better position to express yourself. Then, you will be in a safe space that would allow you to find your light. You too can evolve in a way that enables you to do what you were born to do.

Now let's talk about your light from a cultural point of view. In some ways, the subject of your light and the subject of your culture may be somewhat incompatible. Culture is comprised of attitudes, customs, and beliefs that determine the difference between one group of people from another group of people. Many cultures are dictated by paternal order (male driven). In these cultures, women take a back seat to men. Boys are considered more prominent than girls. In these cases, parents do not look to raise the self-esteem of their boys. The mere fact that they are boys says they are the future leaders of their families whether or not their light is shining.

On the other hand, women and daughters are not looked upon to lead, and the idea of finding their light is of no real significance. Because male roles are clearly defined as leaders and heads of families.

The roles of females are clearly identified in many of the cultures that exist around the world, which over time have taken shape here in America. Women are restricted to support roles in their families. Therefore, the notion of any lights shining in these women are overshadowed by the customs of their respective cultures.

However, as a young person (male or female) in America, the subject of your light may come into play as you become more acclimated to the American way of life. It becomes evident that qualities related to the inner-self become more important due to the fact you become more exposed to the opportunities available to you in the United States of America.

As such, you are more prone to come in to contact with the competitive ways of life in the United States. This lifestyle pulls on you, pressure mounts to achieve more, and the need to have good self-esteem, be more creative, and finding your light become more evident, as you pursue your American dream. With that said, our hope is that this book opens your mind up to the idea of exploring your special talent. So, you can turn your light on to facilitate an easier path to your success while you maintain the customs of your respective cultures.

When your Light does not Shine

Simply stated, if your light does not shine, then you will be living your life in the mode of doing what you have to do. Instead of doing what you were born to do. There is a big difference in that when you do what you have to do, that is what you do to survive. Usually, in those cases, life can be more of a struggle. For example, you work on jobs that you do not like, but you have to survive to take care of a child that you had while you were in high school.

Those jobs usually do not pay very much. Then, you will need to work two jobs in order to earn enough money to pay your bills. Except, as the father of that child you had in high school, you have to pay child support. So, you cannot afford to pay your bills because you have to provide for your child. Therefore, instead of you enjoying life on a college campus, exploring entrepreneurial endeavors, and/or traveling the world with your friends, you live at home with your mother.

Or, you drop out of high school, then you see that it is very hard to find a job because you are not qualified to work anywhere, not even McDonalds. So, you wind up pumping gas to generate some type of cash flow. Then, you might turn to a life of crime in order to survive. Then a few years later, after you figured out that you made some bad decisions, and you are ready to turn your life around, you apply to college with two kids and a criminal record. Perhaps, you might want to explore some other options, however, because of your criminal record, you cannot join the military to pursue your dream to be an officer in the armed forces. Instead, you have to find a job doing anything to meet the requirements of your parole as stipulated by your probation officer.

If you are in a scenario that may lead to sexual relations, and you are a male in high school, do yourself a big favor, use a condom. If you are a female, insist that the male use a condom. Or, postpone that sexual encounter until you are both in a better position to avoid contracting sexually transmitted diseases and/or a teenage pregnancy. Do not let seven (7) minutes of sexual mischief turn into several years of parental strife.

Now, before I go any further, please understand in all that I said about the importance of tuning your light on does not mean you cannot live a good quality of life if you do not turn your light on. What I am saying is that you can live your best life if your light is shining. When your light shines, you feel good, you look good, you do good, you are good to others, you are good to yourself, and you may look for the light in your children. Then, your children can live their best life because they turned on their lights.

The moral of this story is when your light does not shine, you may tend to make bad choices. You tend to follow and not lead. You tend to complain and not create. Most of all, you might miss your true calling, in life, to be what you were born to be. You have a special talent. Make it your business to find out what it is. Then, turn your light on, and let it shine.

Mindfulness and your Light

In addition to what we discussed above to facilitate your ability to understand why your light may not shine, we must discuss one more topic related to jump starting the power of your light.

I would be remiss in my duty if I did not tell you about a very important concept known as mindfulness. You might ask, what is mindfulness? For the record, mindfulness was introduced to mainstream America by Jon Kabat-Zinn. By his definition, mindfulness is purposely paying attention to the present moment without judgment.

In other words, learn how to think less about too many subjects at the same time, which will help you to keep less on your mind about what is happening in real time. Stay in the moment with your thoughts without lending yourself to judgment, negative or other distracting energy related to a particular thought or experience. Instead, stay in tuned to what is happening now. Not what happened yesterday, or what you think will happen tomorrow.

That is not to say that you should not plan for future events or activities. What it says is that you should not add more to your thoughts in dealing with situations that you experience throughout your day. This way of thinking reduces stress, pressure, and anxiety while at the same time, allows you to concentrate more. In addition, it lends to you being able to feel better in that you are not hard pressed by the many thoughts that run through your mind about past, present and future scenarios. Mindfulness provides for a more healthier way of thinking on a daily basis.

Many times, you may find yourself upset about things that have happened to you. Some of those things may be more serious than others. However, depending on the magnitude of those situations will determine how much time you think about those experiences. This may lead to you not feeling good about the thoughts that may lay heavy on your mind.

Mindfulness helps to bring life into focus for you in the moment. Mindfulness can help you to settle down and focus on your life one day at a time. In order to activate your light, this is another method. Whereby, you do not look back and languish on past experiences, which may not do anything to help you feel good about yourself. Mindfulness enables you to build on the energy of your current thoughts without adding or taking away from those thoughts. You focus, you concentrate, and you can get stronger by staying in the moment with one thought at a time.

The issues discussed in this chapter related to some of the bad things we experience that are caused by our family and close family friends compels us to look at the importance of improving our willingness to forgive. Similar to learning how to let go, learning how to forgive provides us with two very essential components of the healing process. When it comes to finding closure to issues and experiences that may have had an impact on our lives, forgiving and letting go will help in a big way. Therefore, in the lab session below, you will be challenged to consider the possibility of forgiving those who may have wronged you in your life.

Why should you learn how to forgive?

As discussed earlier in this chapter, we noted that in some cases, members of our own family along with close family friends could have been responsible for some of our most traumatic life experiences, which contribute to why our light does not shine.

For many of us, it is hard to fathom that our own family member(s) and/or close family friend(s) could be the culprit of such dastardly deeds. However, this book is about overcoming. And, a major component to overcome is to learn how to forgive. When you forgive the person or people who have wronged you, that is not to let them off the hook. Instead, when you forgive, you free yourself from the pain of your past. You free yourself from the anger that you may have carried for a long time, which has not only shackled your ability to feel good about your past, but also may have cast a dark shadow over your life that stifles your joy and happiness.

If you refuse to forgive someone, that is tantamount to denying yourself a chance to live in a new place with a new state of mind. We only live this life one time. Why not give yourself a chance to live your life in a way that leads to you being happy, free of unhappy memories, and release yourself from experiences that only generate feelings that make you sad or mad?

It is also very important to forgive yourself for foolish things you have done and foolish mistakes you have made. We all make mistakes, and we could all learn to feel a lot better if we learn to forgive ourselves.

In addition, it is easy to understand that there may be some people that are hard to forgive. But, that is what makes your willingness to forgive even better. Because the higher the stakes, the better you will feel. Therefore, let's look at some steps below that can assist you on your journey to begin the process of improving your willingness to forgive.

Tips to start the forgiveness process

Have you ever had an experience with a person who did you wrong, and instead of forgiving that person, you completely cut off contact and you do not speak to that person anymore?

Yes_____/No_____

If you answered yes to that question, perhaps now is the time to consider forgiving those who have trespassed against you, so you can move forward with your life. You see, when you leave open wounds that are not healed, you remain stuck in the past. A part of your life is tied to something that cast a shadow over your light. Happy people do not hold on to things like grudges and past experiences that generate negative vibes. Therefore, let's start the process to forgive.

1. If you have begun to take steps to improve your Emotional Intelligence by completing the exercises at the end of each chapter in this book, you are off to a good start in the forgiveness process.

2. The forgiveness process begins when you take steps to improve on yourself and also forgive yourself for the mistakes you have made.

3. As you begin to feel better about yourself, the benefit of that is you also begin to see things about people and your past somewhat differently. You move away from being angry, and you move

toward having a better understanding of yourself and those who have trespassed against you.

4. As time passes, you may never come into contact with those who have wronged you, but still, in your heart you may begin to feel better and allow yourself to forgive, and move on with your life.

5. To forgive is also to let go of past experiences. When you improve your willingness and ability to let go, you should also improve your ability to forgive.

6. To forgive is to allow yourself a chance to live in a more wholesome and happier frame of mind. Continue to work on your self-improvement, then it will be much easier for you to forgive.

To do what you were born to do, you have to turn your light on!

The Bully

in Cyber Space

and your Light...

The bully and you, who can win? OMG! I say, you can win when your light is turned on. It may not sound that simple to you. However, in many ways it really can be that easy. I say that with all due respect and understanding that bullying is a monumental social problem. This is a tough situation that so many young people experience in many different ways. Rather than talk about all of the different types of bullying, I would prefer to talk about the best way to handle any bully situation. For the victims of bullying who have not been able to resolve their respective bully experiences, and for those bully experiences that have ended tragically, I extend my best wishes, respect and concern to those individuals and their families.

With that said, I want to point out that the truth of the matter is most bullies are just as much afraid of you, as you are afraid of them. The only difference is that the bully keeps pushing, and you do not push back. If you pushed back, the bully would retreat. What do I mean when I say push back? What I am saying is you may not have to push back in a physical way. This applies to boys and girls when it comes to bullying.

Instead, it might mean that you stand up for yourself by responding verbally in a way that you can be heard. When you do that, stand up straight, look the bully in the eyes when you are face to face. Now you might say, that is not a good idea.

But, to the contrary, here again, this is where the importance of you having good self-esteem comes into play, and why it is so important that you have good self-esteem. We could say self-esteem is the energy that fuels your light so it can shine. The bottom line is that the best way to not only prevail against bullies, but also not to be targeted by a bully is to improve your self-esteem. Your good self-esteem helps you to shine. Bullies tend not to bother those who feel good about themselves because your positive energy of self is the "Kryptonite" that deters a bully from coming at you. Trust me, bullies know who they should not approach.

Yes, I will admit, in the moment with a bully, that could be a very frightening situation. But, only if you let it escalate to that level. If you check with anybody who has prevailed in their bully experience, you will find that all they probably did was stand up for themselves, and that is enough to let a bully know you are not the one, so keep it moving.

In your mind, the bully may present a large intimidating presence. On the other hand, you may present a much smaller and more timid presence. That smaller presence is better known as your fear. Fear is the biggest reduction of self that there is in a bully related scenario.

To be afraid, is to not give yourself a chance, at all, to succeed in any situation, especially in a scenario where you are bullied. Please know, the real truth about all or most bullies is that they are "Punks." Or not really as tough as they act. Yup, that's right, I said it. Bullies (male and female) are usually less than what they are made out to be. As you may recall, I stated at the beginning of this chapter that typical bullies are afraid of you. They only succeed if you allow yourself to be a victim. Stand up and be heard.

In some cases, a bully might test you to see how far they can get. If they succeed in their attempt to intimidate you, that bully experience will continue.

You have been identified as a target. Therefore, my hope is that when you finish reading this chapter, you complete the work in the self-esteem lab session. Now is the time for you to start the work to improve your self-image so that fuel can inspire you to turn your light on. If that is the case, you will become bully proof. When you have on your "Bully Proof" vest, you give yourself a chance to be strong enough to prevail over any bully whether you are a boy or girl. When your light is on, bullies do not fight the light. Instead, they usually take flight.

Cyber Bullies

To be harassed by bullies in the realm of cyber space is totally unbelievable. It is hard to imagine that someone could have such a significant impact on your life. You cannot see who they are, and you may not even know who they are. In other cases, sometimes you know who is sending you the derogatory messages of hate along with many other distasteful messages to humiliate you. But, what is even more unbelievable and amazing about being bullied in the realm of cyber space is that you allow yourself to be subjected to this painful encouter. Why do you pay so much attention to the messages sent by these people?

When you pay attention to the messages that are intended to humiliate you, then you give those people power over your life. You have to take back your power by first ignoring the negative things that are being said about you, especially when what is being said is not true. And even if it is true, so what. Take responsibility, if warranted, for any part you played in that cyber bully experience. Then, learn from that experience so you do not make the same mistake again.

Take back your power from these people by turning off your devices when you receive the bullying messages. Most of all, the same way you handle a bully as described above, is the same way you handle a bully in cyber space. Although you may not see the cyber bully, you can still stand up. The game is the same, only the players may change.

Therefore, it is imperative that you consider the significant role that good self-esteem can play in helping you prevail in a bully situation. The positive energy you receive due to the love you have for yourself will significantly diminish the effect and influence that any cyber bully could have on you. The focus of this entire book is to stress the importance of how the power of your light increases when you pay more attention to yourself.

Stop venturing into cyber space where you are colliding with UFM's (Unidentified Flying Messages). No need for you to be in a place where you are bullied, insulted, humiliated, and excoriated for being who you are. Come back to earth and explore all of the gifts you have, and the wonderful things about you. Your light is good for any and all situations in life. Please know that it is important for you to understand that life is not what it is, life is what you make it!

When it comes to your light, one of the first steps in the process is to build your self-esteem. It is important to know self-esteem is all about how you see yourself, and how much you value, love and accept yourself. People with good self-esteem are able to feel good about themselves, improve their self-worth and take pride in their skills, abilities, and accomplishments. If you feel your self-esteem is not all it should be, you can improve it.

In the lab session below, you will be called upon to start the process to build yourself up from the inside out. You see, your self-esteem is what drives the energy and passion for your light to shine. Having a strong, humble sense of self will compel you to want to do more because you feel so good. It will be hard for you to stop shining.

The chapter you just completed focused primarily on the fact that a stronger you will improve your chances to deter bullies from coming your way. This lab session will enable you to strengthen your muscles from an emotional perspective in order to feel good enough to stand up for yourself. Please follow the instructions below to start the process.

How to Build Your Self-Esteem

Step One - Take a Self-Esteem Inventory to initiate the process to raise your self-esteem: List five of your strengths and five of your weaknesses. List any strength no matter how small it is. Learn to appreciate your strengths. Then, list two ways you could improve your weaknesses. You can convert your weaknesses into strengths if you work at making yourself better in the areas you list as weaknesses.

Strengths	Weaknesses	Two Ways to Improve your Weaknesses
		1. 2.
		1. 2.
		1. 2.
		1. 2.
		1. 2.

Step Two - Set realistic expectations for yourself. For instance, you can improve your grades if you work harder to achieve that goal. You may not grow to be six feet tall. You can still be a great person who is not six feet tall. You may not have long hair. Then, create great hair styles for short hair.

Step Three - Set aside perfection. No part of your life will ever be totally perfect. Perfection is an artificial creation of society. That type of life does not exist. Instead, focus on your accomplishments as you achieve them.

Step Four – Get to know yourself. Learn more about your basic family tree. Consider what you like to do. Contemplate about what makes you happy. Know that you can do anything. All you have to do is try the things you like to do. Choose to be happy.

Step Five – Be willing to adjust your self-image. Adjust your self-image to match your current skills and abilities, and not those from your past.

Step Six– Stop comparing yourself to others. You do not know as much as you think about those people. You do not know what it is really like to be them. It may not be a good thing to be that person or those people.

Step Seven – Go back to step one. Update your strengths and weaknesses. Work to change weaknesses to strengths, and increase the strength of your strengths by making a note of your accomplishments and daily achievements at school, home, work, when you play sports, or anything else you may be involved with. That way, you will feed yourself a consistent positive message.

Continue to practice these steps on a regular basis until you start to feel that good feeling that comes along with having good self-esteem. That is when you feel good, you look good, you do good, and you realize that you are good. Right here, your light is starting to shine…

Your Relationships and Your Light

As a teenager or even a young adult, relationships can be a very tricky, sticky, confusing and messy subject. For instance, you might have to deal with issues like this. You kiss your boyfriend on Monday, and you see him kiss another girl on Tuesday. You are dating the girl of your dreams, then you find out three weeks later she is cheating on you with the boy of her dreams. You make out with your new boyfriend at his house. He recorded the event and posted it online to show his friends. You break up with your boyfriend, then your best friend is sleeping with him two days later. You like a boy who likes one of your friends. You are dealing with a girl who spends time with you so she can get close to one of your friends.

While walking with your boyfriend, your cell phone rings, he sees that it's another boy who just so happens to be your brother. But your boyfriend is so jealous, he takes your cell phone, accuses you of cheating on him, and he smashes your phone on the sidewalk. Your girlfriend heard from her friends that you like another girl, so she gets her friends together and they jump that girl after school. Now that girl is in the hospital, your girl and her friends get arrested by the police.

You have an argument with your boyfriend. Suddenly, he punches you in the face. He yells and screams at you in public. He accuses you of doing him wrong. Then he tells you that he loves you, and he asks you why did you make me do this to you? You meet a nice girl at a party. She takes your number, and she never calls you.

Your boyfriend says one thing and he does another. He is never on time, and he tends to lie a lot. You break up with your boyfriend or girlfriend, then they call you every day. They show up unannounced at your school, at your house, at your job because they do not accept that you broke up with them. Then, they start fights with your new boyfriend or girlfriend.

You are dating a boy in high school for several months. He tells you every day that he loves you. You tell him that you love him too. You believe that you are in a special relationship with a very special guy. You get pregnant. You tell him that you are pregnant. Then, you never see him again. And, the issues go on and on and on. As you can see, relationships can be a very tricky, sticky, confusing and messy experience. In the above noted scenarios, none of these people described are working with their light on.

It is not that they are bad people because their light may not be turned on, it is just how we behave when we are new to the relationship game. We are learning more about ourselves at this time, and we may not even really know who we are. Having these life experiences will begin to shape your personality. Hopefully, you learn and practice what you should and should not tolerate from other people in relationships.

It is important to know that some people are honest and some people are not. Some people play games and some people do not. There are some people who will deceive you, and there are some people who will mistreat you. However, what you have to do is make sure you are honest with yourself, and recognize early on when someone is not good for you. Move on with your life without a fight, and learn to let go of bad people who cause you to have bad experiences. Learn to live in the positive. Anybody who cannot live there with you, should not be a friend of yours. Remember, in relationships, the negative tends to take down the positive. Do not take your relationship choices for granted.

I wish that when I was your age there was a book like this to shed some light on the complicated subject of relationships. What might be happening to you today happened to me when I was your age. You see, here again, the game is the same only the players have changed. Consequently, I made many bad decisions in my relationship choices. I dated lots of pretty girls, who turned out to be pretty ugly.

Some of them were unhappy for reasons they never talked to me about. Some of them were angry for reasons not caused by me, and some of them did not feel good about themselves at all, which did not allow them to feel good about me. This led to a lot of bad experiences as I tried to treat these young ladies in a special way. But in many cases, they did not seem to be able to appreciate me as a nice guy. Nobody was working with their light on.

This led to friction, misunderstandings, a lack of communication, and they usually dumped me after a short period of time. Back then, I did not understand why things were so tricky, sticky, confusing and messy about my relationship experiences.

I was confused… I thought if a nice boy meets a nice girl, we could live happily ever after. But, I was wrong.

I really did not know what to look for in a girl aside from her good looks. I should have been more interested in the way my girlfriends felt about themselves and the way they behaved towards me instead of how they looked. Not only did I not know what I should be looking for in a choice for my girlfriend, but also, I did not know there was something I should have been looking for aside from their attractive features.

You see, it is a natural part of life to want to be with somebody else to share your life, your love and good experiences. Relationships start, in most cases, because of one person's attraction to another. However, as a teenager, and even in many cases as an adult, you may not be what I call "Relationship Ready."

What does it mean to be Relationship Ready? To be Relationship Ready means that you have good self-esteem, good self-awareness, which means you know who you are and you know something about your basic family tree.

In addition, you have to learn to forgive and let go of bad experiences with bad people. Most of all, you have to learn how to love yourself. As an individual who feels good, you are in a much better position to feel good about somebody else. You would be Relationship Ready. And, your light would be shining.

What happened to me in the above scenarios is that I dealt with some young ladies who did not know who they were; who did not feel good about themselves; who did not let go of bad experiences with bad people; and who did not forgive those who may have hurt them in the past. Their light was not shining, and my light did not shine (30-40 watts) either. I tolerated being mistreated in order to have a relationship with people who were not worthy of my good nature.

I could not find happiness with any girl under those circumstances. And, you will not find any happiness with another person who you meet that has similar issues to those noted above. The tricky thing about this is when you see somebody you are attracted too, they look good to you. However, you cannot see what you really need to see, which would tell you if that person is good for you. We all may look good physically on the outside. But, we all are not emotionally good on the inside… Therefore, take your time. Learn as ~~much~~ as you can about your new girl/boyfriend.

As previously noted, some of us are hurting because of past experiences. Some of us are unhappy due to voids in our lives related to parents we never met. Then there are some of us who are hurting for so many reasons only known to them. That is where another answer lies as to whether or not you have a person who is Relationship Ready. A person who is Relationship Ready is also a person who has not been affected in a negative way by their past experiences. If two people are Relationship Ready, then you have a good chance for a healthy and fun loving relationship.

The important thing to know about any past relationship experiences where you made mistakes, made bad choices, and/or did some things that you are not proud of is that you learn from those experiences. When you learn from your mistakes, accept responsibility for your part, then, hopefully, you will not make the same mistakes again. Sometimes, you may even have to forgive yourself.

Based on the ups and downs of my relationship experiences, I learned to get better by first realizing that I need to improve my own self-worth. Then, I realized that instead of being attracted to how a person looks on the outside, I made it my business to find out how attractive an attractive person is on the inside. There is an old saying that says, "Beauty is skin deep." Not only that, relationships are supposed to be good. In order to make your relationships good, you too have to be good. You make yourself good by having the good qualities of self-esteem, self-awareness, and self-love.

Most of all, I learned that it is very important to let go of bad memories of bad relationships with people who were not worthy of my love. This helped me to be a better person in my next relationship, and it helped me to clear my mind so I could make room to feel good about my new mate. It is important to bring a clean heart and open mind to that person in the future who deserves to get the best of you.

When you feel good, you are willing to communicate with your partner about how you feel on any subject. In addition, when you have the qualities noted above, you tend to feel more secure about yourself, and you do not bring negative energy like jealousy, insecurity and violent tendencies to your relationships. You will know that you are in a good relationship with your guy or girl when they demonstrate love and respect for you on a consistent basis.

In case you still do not understand the important connection between good relationships and good self-esteem, good self-awareness, and the importance of loving yourself, please consider this in case you ask the question: Why do I need to have good self-esteem, self-awareness, and love myself to be in a relationship? The answer is because these elements provide you with the capabilities you will need to handle the good, the bad, and the ugly aspects of your relationship experiences.

The hope is that all of your relationships will be good, happy and fun loving experiences. However, the reality is that may not always be the case. Therefore, in the event that you find yourself in a bad relationship with another person, it would behoove you to be prepared to handle the emotional turbulence that may arise, and find your way out of that relationship. See, if you know better, then you could and you should do better.

There is an old saying that says, "Only the strong survive." That does not mean you survive because you are physically strong with muscles bulging out all over your body. What that means is that when you are strong emotionally, with good self-esteem, good self-awareness, resilience, and you love yourself, that is the kind of strength you will need to survive during some of your most challenging life experiences you might have in and out of relationships. Therefore, with these qualities, not only will you improve your chances to prevail emotionally, but also you will improve your chances to find good healthy and loving relationships.

What you should know about relationships is that they are supposed to be good. Just like all of your friendships, they too should be good. Love is an action, not a word. For instance, a person should not mistreat you, beat you, cheat on you, and then tell you that they love you. Love is not supposed to hurt.

Love should be demonstrated by two people doing nice things for one another that generate good feelings that lead to happiness. If love hurts, you do not have love. You have pain!

When it comes to your light, when it shines bright, you will be able to make better choices in your relationship endeavors. You will not be interested in people who walk in the dark. Your light helps you move away from individuals whose light is not on. Your light will attract you to others whose lights are on as well. All of those aforementioned tricky, sticky, confusing and messy scenarios will become a thing of the past.

With your light, not only do you learn how to have good relationships with others, but also you will learn how to have a good relationship with yourself. Use your light, and let it shine bright for you to make your way to happiness, success, abundance, and self-fulfillment.

To prepare yourself for the inexplicable relationship experiences you may have during your journey through your teen-age and young adult-life, you should look at yourself in the mirror. Say to yourself, "I love me some me." Learn to love yourself. When you see yourself in the mirror, say positive things about yourself so you can learn to love yourself more and more each day. To make this work, you have to understand that this is a process. You have to do this more than one time. Tell yourself that you can do anything, all you have to do is try, and you believe it because it's true.

When you have a good self-image, it helps you to move away from the relationship experiences noted above into more healthy relationships with people who also feel good about themselves, as well.

By now you should have worked through several lab session exercises in this book. Let's do some relationship role plays to check your Relationship Readiness.

Role Play Relationship Scenarios: What would you do?

1. You see your boyfriend/girlfriend kissing somebody else on the steps at school while you are returning to class from the bathroom.

2. Your girlfriend/boyfriend cell phone rings and the picture of another boy/girl appears on the screen. They start talking and laughing while you are standing there.

3. Your boyfriend/girlfriend cheated on you. That person apologized and wants you back. Would you take that person back and why?

4. Your boyfriend/girlfriend breaks up with you for no reason. He/she just ended the relationship and will not tell you why.

5. You notice that your girlfriend/boyfriend tends to lie a lot especially about things that are important to you.

6. You meet a nice girl/boy who is smart, helps you with your school work, treats you really special, and wants to spend more time with you.

7. You make out with your boyfriend at his house. He records the event and posts it online.

8. You and your boyfriend are having an argument. He is angry that another boy called you. Suddenly, he grabs you, and slaps you in the face.

9. You find out that your girlfriend/boyfriend cheated on you with your best friend.

10. Your boyfriend/girlfriend argue a lot. You realize that you two do not think alike on issues that are very important to you.

The aforementioned scenarios are intended to present you with relationship situations that compel you to make smart decisions to ensure that you learn to keep the focus on you. In addition, just to make sure you stay on the right track, below you will see Relationship Scenarios that you can use as examples to know when you are in a good or bad place during your relationship journeys.

Good Relationship Scenarios:

Two people show respect and love towards one another on a daily basis.

Two people communicate their true feelings on any subject to one another.

Two people stay committed to one another, and do not cheat on one another.

Under no circumstance, do two people allow intimate partner violence into their relationship.

Two people demonstrate their love by doing loving things to make each other happy.

Two people may realize their relationship is not working. They agree to go their own way and remain friends for a lifetime.

Two people get married; build a life together; and make a family.

In the above relationship scenarios, both people are letting their light shine. They find it easy to love one another because there are no unresolved personal issues blocking the way to their happiness.

Bad Relationship Scenarios:

One or both people lack self-esteem, self-awareness, and self-love.

One or both people are very jealous and insecure.

One or both people lack trust in one another.

One or both people have cheated on the other.

One or both people do not talk about their feelings.

One or both people uses intimate partner violence to control the relationship.

One or both people abuses drugs and alcohol.

In these relationship scenarios, they would be considered dysfunctional and unhealthy relationships. These relationship scenarios do not generate any positive, productive, and healthy loving relationship experiences.

These relationship scenarios are driven by a myriad of bad experiences that can lead to constant bickering, violence, and your overall unhappiness with people who behave as described.

Remember, you only live once. Do not take your relationship choices for granted. Always choose good over bad. Happiness is a choice. Choose to be happy!!!

In addition to talking about good and bad relationship scenarios, and how you could and should prepare yourself for relationships by ensuring that you have good self-esteem, good self-awareness, and strong love for yourself, we must also discuss a very important topic related to relationships. As much as you strive to have good relationships with others, you also have to prepare for what happens on the other end of the spectrum of relationships, and that is when your relationships end.

Sometimes, you might decide to end your relationship with another person. Then there are times the other person might end their relationship with you. In this case, you will experience the ramifications of rejection. To be rejected can be surprising, depressing, shocking and most of all unexpected. If you engage in any type of relationship during your lifetime, I guarantee that you will experience some form of rejection. What is important here is not that you were rejected, but how you handled being rejected by another person.

To assist you with this somewhat difficult experience, below there are some steps you can take to create a less painful journey through your experiences with rejection. The next session may be tough, but as you will find out, you will learn a lot from this information. It will only make you a better person, and that is what we all should want to be.

 ## How to handle being Rejected?

One of the risks of engaging in relationships is that at some point, the relationship may end and you may be rejected. Rejection could be defined as another person refuses to continue their relationship with you.

There is no doubt being rejected can be a blow to a person's ego. Such a blow could lead to emotional turbulence-anger, sadness, depression and despair. Or, if you remain positive about being rejected, it could be like hitting a speed bump before you start a new chapter in your life.

However, too often, for many of us, rejection may lead to emotional challenges, which prolong the intensity of the rejection. This perspective of rejection may keep your life in limbo. Unless you are a robot, you will experience an emotional reaction to being rejected. Rejection can hurt, and depending on how you are rejected and the reason for being rejected, that will determine how long you will allow yourself to experience the pain of rejection.

Essentially, how you deal with rejection depends on your view of your past experiences. In addition, it will include your understanding of rejection and how you see yourself. Please know that everybody who goes through life will experience rejection in one way or another. Everyday people are rejected by family members, lovers, employers, and friends. As much as it may hurt, rejection is a regular part of everyday life.

Therefore, it would behoove you to not allow yourself to be derailed into extended periods of self-pity with negative emotions. Remember, you still have a life to live, love to give, and love to receive.

I think you should know that it is a colossal waste of your time to focus on the person who rejected you. It would be more productive to realize that life is about you and what makes you happy. You cannot change the person who rejected you. However, you can change your behavior. You can do that by focusing on you. Be aware of your thoughts and actions in the midst of being rejected.

For instance, are you thinking that you are no good because somebody declared they no longer want you in their life? Are you consumed with anger and thoughts of getting back at somebody? Do you spend countless hours devising plans to hurt the person who rejected you?

If you answered yes to any of the questions above, then you are consumed by some counter-productive behavior and you will only intensify your feelings of rejection. Below are five things you can do when you are faced with rejection.

1. Be real with yourself.

    Try to look at how being rejected has affected you. More specifically, determine what emotion the rejection is stimulating within you. You may feel anger, but try to determine what emotion is beneath your anger. Admit you are feeling sad because you were rejected. Talk to a family member or a close friend about your real feelings. If you hide from your real feelings, you will only complicate the issues, which may lead to other problems.

2. Deal with your feelings.

    Often, we run from our feelings. We should sit with our feelings so we can actually experience our feelings. When you sit with your feelings, and allow yourself to feel that specific emotion, you have a chance to take control of your emotions. Then, you can determine how to handle your emotions.

3. See your rejection as a learning opportunity.

   Being rejected can be one of the best learning opportunities you can experience. Pay attention and try to learn from that experience. If you are rejected by a significant other (boyfriend/girlfriend), do not blame the other person. You may not get much out of that process.

   However, if you think about what you could have done differently, you may be on to something. Rejection can be a great time for self-reflection. This will give you a chance to take a look at how you may have contributed to being rejected.

   If the truth be told, we all participate in some way or another in every rejection we experience in our lives. If you can determine how you contributed to being rejected, the rejection can serve as a valuable learning experience to prevent future rejection.

4. Explore your childhood upbringing.

   We all have been rejected at some point as a child. If you were ridiculed and judged when you were rejected as a child, as an adult, you may see rejection as humiliating and shameful.

   However, if you were taught that rejection is a part of everyday life, as an adult you may not be troubled when you face rejection. What messages did you receive as a child when you were faced with rejection? We tend to act out as adults based on messages we learned as children. The good news is you can re-program your messages.

   Then, you can replace these messages with healthy productive messages. For example, you can allow yourself to understand and accept that rejection is a part of life. More importantly, you can handle rejection.

5. Allow yourself to experience personal growth.

   What would happen if you were never rejected? Would you grow as a human being? Do you need to grow?

   If everyone said yes to you, then you would not need to change anything. You would not have to learn anything. That would lead to a boring life. Being rejected and criticized, in most cases, is an opportunity for you to grow. Resisting or hiding from rejection is an exercise in futility.

   Learning from rejection can be fruitful and lead to personal growth. Take the time now to see what lesson you learned from being rejected. What did you learn about yourself? What commitment can you make to yourself in future endeavors as a result of the lessons you learned from being rejected?

Your Parents,  Your Family

and Your Light

The interesting thing about this life we live is that we do not get to choose the families we are born into. As previously discussed earlier in this book, some of us are born into families where there is a mommy and daddy who are married. Some of us are born into families where there is a mommy and a step father or a daddy and a step mother. Then, on the other hand, some of us are born into families where there is a mommy and no daddy. In other cases, there is a mommy and daddy, but they are your adopted parents or foster parents. Also, some of us are born into families where our grandmothers play the role of our mother and father. Finally, some of us are born into families where one of our parents either dies due to illness or dies all of sudden.

This is the case for all of us as human beings when it comes to our family life. And, you should know that it is only by chance that we are born into our families no matter what the race, creed, religion or color is regarding your particular family. With that said, there are some things about family life I think you should know from the adult perspective. My hope is that it will clear the way to make your family life easier to understand, and less complicated in your life experience.

In other words, try to understand what I am saying through the eyes of somebody else beyond your own understanding who has more life experience than you. Perhaps, you might want to consider me to be your imaginary friend "The Guru." The more you know and the better you understand your family life based on my teachings, I believe it will be easier for you to realize that you too were born with a special talent no matter what type of family you were born into. You have to know that everything is going to be alright. Just give yourself a chance no matter what your family circumstance.

You and your Parent's Divorce

As a child, you may see your life with your mother and father as a wonderful thing. You have so many memories of good times together with your parents. However, what you might not see are the difficulties your parents experience in their relationship.

In some cases, our parents do not get along. But, they try to stay married for the children. Parents tend to argue when they stay married and they do not get along. Sometimes arguments lead to fights. The constant tension and conflict tends to turn people away from one another.

There are so many reasons why our parent's divorce. They divorce because of finances, because of infidelity, they grow a part, domestic violence, and even disagreement about how to raise their children. But, you should know, whatever the reasons are between your parents that led to their divorce, those issues were not your fault. When parents break up, it is not because of the children. At some point, adults come to realize that life might be better for all concerned, including you, if they split and went their own way.

As a result, you wind up in what we call a "Broken home." Of course, you, and perhaps your brothers and sisters are all left broken hearted due to the absence in the house of one of your parents. In some cases, you might even be mad at the parent who you believe caused the divorce. Nevertheless, whatever the cause of the breakup between your parents, you should realize that it is between your parents. Their divorce does not change their love for you. It only changes how and when they will see you in order to spend time together.

Therefore, the divorce of your parents does not have to be the end of the world for you. In fact, their divorce can be the beginning of a new world for you. There are so many new opportunities that can arise for you when your parent's divorce. Who knows, you might get your own room in your father's new house. You might get to spend more time with one of your parents. You might make friends and have great relationships with your new step brothers and sisters that come into play with your parent's next relationship. I am not saying that divorce is a good thing. What I am saying is do not make divorce a bad thing. Give yourself a chance to see the brighter side of things.

You and your Step Parent

When your parents do not spend their entire life together, more than likely your father will meet a new girlfriend and your mother will meet a new boyfriend. That is just the way life is. Eventually, your parents may or may not marry their new significant other. However, over time, that new person in either one of your parent's life may now become your Step Parent. If they are together, and they seem to be happy, then either one of your parents are in a good place with their new mate.

In those situations, sometimes you as the child may not be happy about your respective parent's new relationship. You may have some feelings like that person is going to take your parent away from you.

Or, your parent will not give you the love and attention that you want. In reality, more than likely, that is not the case. Your parent's love has not changed for you. That parent has found somebody they can love in addition to you. And, if for some strange reason, you decide that you do not like your Step Parent because he "Ain't your father and/or she ain't your mother" that only makes your new family life more difficult for you.

It is important to understand that you do not have to like your Step Parent. It would be nice, but you should respect that person. He/she is an adult, and good people respect their elders. If you love your parent who has found somebody to help make them happy, then you should show respect for your Step Parent. Eventually, if you give that person a chance, I bet you too will come to be happy about your Step Parent.

You must understand that when your parents find a new mate, they do it in an effort to meet somebody that will make them happy. They may not take into consideration what makes you happy about their new mate. You see, as a child, you will grow up and move on with your life. So, while you are out living your life, your parents try to seek and find some happiness for their own lives.

As a parent, it is better to grow old with a partner, especially since your children will be living their own lives, raising their families without much time to check on mom, or dear old dad. With some of this, you may not come to understand until you become an adult. Once you begin to experience a break up in your own relationships, it will be easier for you to understand what happened to your parents. Believe me, if you date, you will experience a break up. Learn to respect and support your parent in their relationship with their new mate.

As a matter of fact, not all relationships last forever. Breaking up is hard to do at times. The reality is that breaking up, making up, and finding new relationships is a regular part of the life we live. You should always strive to be happy with yourself and to be happy in any friendship or relationship that you have with another person.

You, and no Father in your Life

Life without your father can be a difficult life experience to handle. There is no question about it. Anybody would wonder, why their father is not involved in their life? What is wrong with me? How come my father does not want me? Those are some very tough questions to answer. Unfortunately, only the person who is your father, and who has not been a part of your life can answer your specific questions as to why he is not in your life.

Since your questions may not have been answered, and there is no father present in your life, that, in many cases, can cause you to become angry. You may tend to act out. Join gangs. Take drugs. Be hostile towards your mother. Or, lead you to a life of crime and violence. I know this to be true because of all the stories I have heard from young men and women who never met their fathers. The reality is that there are so many reasons why our fathers are not involved in our lives. So much so, that could be the title for another book.

You may not care about all of those reasons. You only want to know why your father has not come to see about you. As I said earlier, and I will say it again. This is not your fault. What do I mean when I say it is not your fault? In other words, I mean that you did not cause your father to abandon you. For his own reasons, good or bad, your father is not in your life.

 If I could offer you any way to feel better regarding the pain you experienced in connection to the void in your life created by the absence of your father, I would suggest that you try to forgive the person who is your father. Although you may not ever know who he is, the act of forgiveness would serve as a healing process for you.

After all, at this point, have you already spent enough time being mad about your father? Ask yourself, how has that worked out for you? Is your life any better or worse? What have you gained? After all of this time, if you never meet your father, it would not be a good idea for you to be mad about that for the rest of your life. If you carry your anger for a lifetime, you will not give yourself a chance to live your own life in a happy and healthy way.

You would not be able to turn your light on. You are here for a reason. You need to believe that. Do not forget you still have to live the life you have to create a bright future for you and your future family.

I want you to know that there is nothing wrong with you. Try not to be angry about something that is totally out of your control. Instead, see if you can focus on trying to let go of an issue that may have caused you a lot of pain in your life. Remember, life is supposed to be good. Sometimes the way our life starts out does not make us feel special. But, if you take control of your feelings about this issue, you could start the work to make sure the rest of your life is very special.

If I may suggest, if you are interested in finding your father, or learning something about him, today, because of technology there are so many websites and outlets that you can use to increase the possibly for you to locate your father. So, all is not lost. It is up to you. You can change this situation from a negative to a positive.

Another good thing about your situation is that you were born with a special talent. That light of yours does not come from your parents. Your light comes from the natural order of things in the universe. Although you do not have your father, you do have your light. Turn it on, and let it shine everywhere you go. Talk to people about the way you feel. You will feel better.

You and your Adopted/Foster Parents

Just like in the case above, growing up without your parents could be a very hurtful and traumatic experience. Quite often, when you are adopted, you may not find out until later on in life after you fell in love with your adopted parents that they, in fact, are not your biological parents. What a gigantic shock that can be for any person who has no idea that the people they knew to be mommy and daddy are not really their mother and father. OMG!

While on the other hand, growing up with foster parents, changing homes and families on a regular basis, and living in group homes while knowing that your mother and father did not take care of you, as they should have as your parents. What a way to start your life.

The recipe for success in any of these family scenarios are the same. You are born into your family life circumstance. You are either affected in a way that can inspire you to be what you were born to be. Or, you are defected by rejecting your family life circumstance. Then, you fall victim to the dark side of how these experiences can make you feel. And, you build a wall filled with all kinds of emotional turmoil to block out the world that presents you with the same opportunities as any child born into what might seem like a normal household with their biological mother and father.

However, if you read all of the aforementioned family life situations that we are born into, you would have learned that we are all born into families that cause every one of us to deal with some type of issues that can interfere with our path to happiness. Therefore, do some research, and you will find that there are so many entertainers, athletes, preachers, teachers, doctors, lawyers, and comedians who grew up just like you with either adopted or foster parents. The only difference between you and them is they chose to find a better life for themselves. What about you? Can you find a way to turn your light on so you do not have to walk around in the dark due to the pain you feel about your family life circumstance? Talk to people about the way you feel. You are not alone.

You and your Grandmother

If you are being raised by your grandmother, that is usually because your parents for one reason or another are not in the best position to take care of you. The good thing is that you are still connected to your family. Hopefully, you have some ties to your mother and your father. If not, you are in a good place with your grandmother. In most cases, with your grandmother, she will provide you with an abundance of good values that were in effect when she was your age. Your grandmother wants the best for you. She has raised one of your parents, and she may be a little tired right now. But, show her love and respect. Do what she says.

Instead of wondering why your parents are not taking care of you, spend some time to find out more about you, and what you like to do in life so you can activate that light of yours. More than likely, your grandmother knows a lot about your family life. She can fill in the blanks to a lot of questions you might have. Talk to your grandmother so you can fill in some of the blanks, and brighten up your light. Then, it would only be a matter of time before you are taking care of your grandmother. And, you know that would make her very happy.

You and the Death of a Parent

This, like all of the scenarios noted above, the death of a parent is devastating. I can say that because my mother died all of sudden when I was only nine years old.

Then, as I told you earlier, my oldest sister overdosed on heroin, and she died three years later when I was 12 years old. So, I am very familiar with the devastating effects of the deaths of close family members.

However, one thing we must understand about this life we live; as sure as we are born, we are going to die. Usually, death does not send you a text or an email to let you know what date you should expect to die. Death can happen to you and/or anybody you love on any given day and time. And, yes, it always hurts when a loved one dies.

I cannot tell you how to mourn the loss of your loved ones. But, what I will tell you is that our parents, grandparents and other loved ones understand life and death as we all should. What I mean by that is parents, grandparents and others do not want you to stop living because they passed away. Instead, they would want you to live and be thankful you had them in your life. Now you have to carry the torch and spread the goodwill of your family.

It is one thing to mourn and feel very sad about your loss. It is another thing to spiral out of control due to the loss of a loved one, and not be able to move forward with your life. Your loved ones who have passed away would want the best for you. You should not want to let them down by allowing yourself to lose control and ruin your life due to the death of a loved one.

What is important for you to remember is that light of yours will always shine. It will shine as long as you live. The light is what shows you your way out of darkness. Turn it on, let it shine, and remember your family members loved you, and they want you to be all that you can be.

So, if the truth be told, we do not choose the families we are born into. As previously discussed in this chapter, family life comes in a wide variety of combinations. Some of those combinations seem like the perfect set up for family life. Some of those combinations may seem like the most imperfect set up for family life. Please understand, based on what you know now, you can see that sometimes the perfect family life combination may be hard to find. So, learn to appreciate and love your family combination. Now that you have read this book, hopefully you have a better understanding of why you should embrace your family life. Simply because, no matter what it is, you were born with a special talent. Therefore, make the best of your family life combination. Then, turn on your light and let it shine.

As you move to the lab session below, you should have some fun. Now we are going to talk about a subject everybody should like. That is the fun subject about learning to love yourself. Why is that a fun subject? Because it can be so easy to love yourself.

After all, why would you not love yourself? You were born for a reason, and your family combination does not determine your destination in life.

Therefore, improve your love of self, and the rest will come easy for you. Read the passages below and make them a part of your thinking on a daily basis.

Learn to Love Yourself, aka: Self-Love – Meditate on This...

Self-love is necessary for you to function successfully in your everyday life. Self-love can pick you up when you are feeling down. "If you love yourself, you will never be alone."

It is the key to the happiness that you should feel inside about you, your life, and the people you come in contact with on a daily basis.

One of the most important aspects of self-love is that it can serve as the glue to hold you together during tough times, sad times, and any other challenging life situation. There is so much more to self-love and the enormous benefits of self-love are described below.

This rendition of self-love was contributed by Ms. Doris M. Wheeler-Harmon, who I met at the Harlem Book Fair in July 2009.

Love Yourself...

You must really learn to love yourself in order to enjoy your life. Respect yourself, value who you are and then you will be ready to love others in a healthy and good way.

Self-Love...

As children, we should have been taught early how to give love to ourselves in a real way. We would have learned how to understand and keep ourselves out of depression. We should delight in who we are, keep ourselves healthy and forgive ourselves for wrong turns. Love for self will take away the blame, the guilt, anger and shame. Healthy self-love builds you up on the inside out and keeps you strong during hard and challenging times.

Positive Self-Love...

Self-Love is a project we should all strive towards. Loving yourself is the starting point towards love for others. Only you control how much love you receive. Do you talk down to yourself or do you allow yourself to laugh, relax and be at peace? Do you make yourself feel anxious and evil or do you sit quietly with self and allow love to flow in? Only you can love yourself the way you really need. One of the most important lessons in life is… how to love yourself and value who you are.

You begin to enjoy life itself because you enjoy the person you are always with…yourself! Look in the mirror. The person looking back at you deserves your love, your care and your respect. Smile at your best friend.

No matter what you know about yourself and no matter what has happened to you, the person in the mirror has gone through it with you. Love the person you are looking at.

Say I love you to yourself…everyday…loving yourself is a cup only you can fill.

Always remember, before you can have a good relationship with another person, you should first have a good relationship with yourself. Learn to love yourself. Get to know yourself, and be good to yourself at all times. When you make that connection with yourself, you can make a much better connection with someone else.

Did you enjoy learning about the importance of love for yourself? If you can put this all together, which I believe you can and will do, you are on your way to living a good life no matter where you come from and no matter how your life started. Remember, "What is important is not how we start, what matters most is how we finish."

You have arrived. Turn your light on, and let it shine!

Thank you for the time you took to read this book! Please tell somebody you know to tell somebody they know; to tell somebody she knows; to tell somebody he knows; to tell somebody they all know about this book.

Then, we can help our children be who and what they were born to be, and make the world a better place for you and me.

Edwards Brothers Malloy
Ann Arbor MI. USA
September 11, 2017